ZEN IN THE AGE OF ANXIETY

ALSO BY TIM BURKETT

Nothing Holy about It:
The Zen of Being Just Who You Are

Zen in the Age of Anxiety

WISDOM FOR NAVIGATING OUR MODERN LIVES

Tim Burkett

EDITED BY WANDA ISLE

SHAMBHALA · Boulder · 2018

Shambhala Publications, Inc.
4720 Walnut Street
Boulder, Colorado 80301
www.shambhala.com

9 8 7 6 5 4 3 2 1

First Edition
Printed in the United States of America

♾ This edition is printed on acid-free paper that meets the
American National Standards Institute z39.48 Standard.
♻ This book is printed on 30% postconsumer recycled paper.
For more information please visit www.shambhala.com.
Distributed in the United States by Penguin Random House LLC
and in Canada by Random House of Canada Ltd

Library of Congress Cataloging-in-Publication Data
Names: Burkett, Tim, author. | Isle, Wanda, editor.
Title: Zen in the age of anxiety: wisdom for navigating our modern lives /
    Tim Burkett; edited by Wanda Isle.
Description: First Edition. | Boulder: Shambhala, 2018. | Includes index.
Identifiers: LCCN 2017040620 | ISBN 9781611804867 (pbk.: alk. paper)
Subjects: LCSH: Zen Buddhism. | Anxiety—Religious aspects—Zen
    Buddhism.
Classification: LCC BQ9268.6 .B87 2018 | DDC 294.3/927—dc23
LC record available at https://lccn.loc.gov/2017040620

Dedicated to all who aspire to tap into what T. S. Eliot called "the still point of the turning world."

It's not as far off as you think!

Contents

Editor's Introduction

CHAPTER ONE
I walk down the street.
 There is a deep hole in the sidewalk.
 I fall in.
 I am lost . . . . I am helpless.
  It isn't my fault.
It takes forever to find a way out.

CHAPTER TWO
I walk down the same street.
 There is a deep hole in the sidewalk.
 I pretend I don't see it.
 I fall in again.
I can't believe I am in this same place.
  But, it isn't my fault.
It still takes me a long time to get out.

CHAPTER THREE
I walk down the same street.
 There is a deep hole in the sidewalk.

I see it is there.
I still fall in . . . it's a habit . . . but,
   my eyes are open.
   I know where I am.
It is *my* fault.
I get out immediately.

CHAPTER FOUR
I walk down the same street.
   There is a deep hole in the sidewalk.
   I walk around it.

CHAPTER FIVE
I walk down another street.

—PORTIA NELSON

WALKING DOWN A DIFFERENT STREET is not about changing what we do or how we do it. It is about changing what and how we think. It requires a new approach to life—and that is what this book offers.

Is this book for you? A glance at the table of contents may tell you.

Part One, Wounding and Splintering, looks at the primary causes of pain and confusion in our culture. The title reflects the fact that our deeply ingrained way of thinking about and responding to frustrations, disappointments, and setbacks wounds not only us but also those around us. We are not isolated beings living isolated lives. When we fall into a hole, we take others with us.

In this first section, author Tim Burkett writes about the split between the heart and mind, and the inevitable splintering of the psyche that follows. Splintering is the source of our deepest pain. One by one, Tim discusses the areas that cause the most splintering: feelings of inadequacy and self-loathing, issues related to sex and to money, and the stigma associated with failure. Often we are so splintered we feel as if we're moving through life alone, in a trance-like state, unaware of the abundance that is fundamental to our interdependent nature.

Part Two, Suturing and Healing, introduces an ancient wisdom that offers a different approach to life. Unlike many wisdom teachers today, Tim doesn't use obscure or ambiguous language of the past, choosing instead images and metaphors drawn from our own popular culture. The last chapter of the book, "Living and Dying in a State of Readiness," delves unflinchingly into our greatest anxiety, revealing how even the fear of death can be bridged.

The first nine chapters each contain a Key, short enough to use as a mantra or to write on a sticky note for your refrigerator. A section called Doing the Work ends each chapter. You will begin to experience life in a different way as you engage these ancient teachings, personally and intimately.

In the epilogue, Tim offers some final thoughts about the common thread connecting the world's major religions and traditions. It's the same thread that can suture and heal our splintered hearts—and that can also heal our world.

An ancient wisdom says if you pull a single thread, a whole world comes into being. May that world be a compassionate one.

—WANDA ISLE
Editor

PART ONE

Wounding and Splintering

The significant problems we face cannot be solved at the same level of thinking we were at when we created them.

—ALBERT EINSTEIN

ONE

Being Human

I can't get no satisfaction
'Cause I try and I try and I try and I try
I can't get no, I can't get no
Satisfaction

THE ROLLING STONES's first big hit in the United States was "(I Can't Get No) Satisfaction" and is still considered by many the greatest song they ever recorded. It made the charts in 1965. I was in my fourth year at Stanford University, on the supposed fast track to success and happiness. I'd been born into an upper middle class family, I lived in the beautiful and prestigious San Francisco Bay Area, and I never gave more than a moment's thought to the concerns about money and economic status that the previous generation had worried about during the post–World War Two era.

So you may be wondering why the lyrics of that classic Stones song would resonate so deeply with me and my generation. The reason is that, in the sixties, there was more going on than just the restless angst of a privileged generation. Younger Americans were among the first to deeply question the decisions coming out of Washington and the aggressive international path our country had taken. The anguish and actions of college students and other young people around the country polarized the nation: Peace activists (including me) rallied against the Vietnam War while returning soldiers, with mangled bodies and war-weary eyes, were honored in parades and then forgotten. Angry and often violent polarization was reflected on streets and campuses, in our art, and in our music.

And that man comes on the radio
He's tellin' me more and more
About some useless information
Supposed to fire my imagination

The idea of the American dream, so fulfilling to my parents and grandparents, no longer nourished the hearts and minds of many in my generation. I tried, and I tried, and I tried, but I got no satisfaction—not as a peace activist, or a student, or at my job. I got a little satisfaction in love, but then we broke up. A little satisfaction from sex, but it didn't last very long.

A year before "Satisfaction" came on my radio, I'd begun a meditation practice with Suzuki Roshi at the San Francisco Zen Center. For a while my heart was calm and peaceful, but when the dissatisfaction returned, it seemed deeper and more impenetrable than ever.

Meditation doesn't save us from life's trials and tragedies. In fact, Zen meditation allows us to enter completely both the joy and darkness that make up this great life. Deep healing often begins in darkness, in times when we feel deep dissatisfaction and little or no vitality.

The place of our deepest fears can be rich soil when it is entered into fully. As our eyes adjust to the dark, clear-seeing becomes possible. Standing firm in the darkness, without withdrawing or lashing out, we discover what motivates us in healthy, wholesome ways and what drives us to exhaustion and depression. We see for ourselves how fear-based thinking and emotional reactivity influence us individually and collectively. Fear is used by us and against us, and recognizing this truth is the first step toward healing.

This book offers an approach to life that opens us up to a new way of thinking and being in the world. The approach is not new, but too often confusing language, unfamiliar metaphors, and practices that confound and bewilder obscure it. This book is written in the style of an owner's manual, a guide to being human, and begins by focusing on the four most troublesome areas that most of us are intimately familiar with: feelings of unworthiness, and issues surrounding sex, money, and failure. These are the outermost layers of the onion, and they must be penetrated with clear-seeing, generosity, and openness.

Year after year,
the monkey's face
wears a monkey's mask

—BASHO, SEVENTEENTH CENTURY

Basho's poem points to the difficulty of penetrating the onion by seeing through our fear-based thinking. But as I stayed with my meditation practice, I began to see through the layers to realize a direct correlation between the fear-based dramas playing out in my mind and my can't-get-no-satisfaction life. Maybe you can, too.

ONE STEP AT A TIME: THE FOOTPRINT STAGE OF PRACTICE

Every major religion includes contemplative practices that can move us beyond the confusion, disintegration, longing, and weariness associated with fear-based thinking. Often, however, we have to completely exhaust ourselves before we are ready to embark on this life-altering path.

Here in the United States, we are exhausting ourselves at a younger and younger age. I was twenty when I began my meditation practice. Meditation was an oddity then. But today more and more people are turning to this ancient practice to cope with the mental and emotional stress and weariness that have become hallmarks of American culture.

Maybe you've tried to meditate in the past but have lost your way and quit—perhaps repeatedly. It's not an uncommon experience. Often people read or hear something inspiring and begin a regular practice. They've caught a glimpse of something meaningful, like rabbit tracks on the surface of new-fallen snow. But then the deeper teachings that support the practice become remote and incomprehensible, and the footprints fade away like tracks vanishing in falling snow.

This is what I call the footprint stage of practice. When the tracks disappear, people become overwhelmed or discouraged and withdraw back into their frenzied life of dissatisfaction. Later, the tracks reappear, and for a time, the path is clearly marked. Repeatedly the footprints seem to disappear and reappear.

Eventually, you'll come to realize that the tracks are everywhere—but always, the snow keeps falling and covering them up. Life is continuously unfolding in unlikely and unpredictable ways. Repeatedly, we seem to drift back into the dramas, anxieties, and worries of a fear-driven life. But this, too, may be the path. Each time we return, we are a little wiser and a little more sure-footed as we realize that the path is right where we are, even when the footprints fade from view. When the footprints are visible, we feel secure; when they vanish, we learn to trust. Even though the path is always here, the way we walk it is uniquely our own.

In 2015, forty-five years after I moved away from the Bay Area, I went back to promote my first book, *Nothing Holy about It*. One afternoon, I walked to Bush Street where the San Francisco Zen Center had been. It was now a senior center.

As I stood on the corner of Bush and Laguna, my mind was flooded with memories. I had practiced at the center for five years, from 1964 to 1969, with Suzuki Roshi, who became one of the most famous Zen teachers in the world. Five years may not seem like a long time to absorb Suzki's teachings, but in the days before he was famous he had only a handful of devoted students, so I saw him frequently.

Thinking back to those days, I looked through a window into the room where the auditorium used to be, where on Saturday evenings Suzuki watched imported movies with his Japanese congregation. Then on Sunday mornings he would give dharma talks for his small group of American students. The Japanese congregation didn't meditate or go to his dharma talks. In Japan, only the monks living in monasteries meditated and studied the teachings.

Each day as I entered the building for morning meditation, I passed a giant poster advertising the upcoming movie. A typical poster featured swords dripping with blood, decapitated limbs, and geishas in distress. These looked like pretty lousy movies by my standards. When I wanted some entertainment, I went to North Beach, where they showed artistic movies that had some depth and were emotionally moving. I felt bad that my teacher had to watch those B-rated imports.

One Sunday morning Suzuki looked tired.

"Do you have to watch movies every Saturday night?" I asked.

"Oh, yes," he said, cheerfully. "We watch movies together on Saturday nights."

"I'm sorry you have to watch those movies. Do you like *any* of them?" I asked.

"I like them all," he said.

He liked them all? Apparently my teacher was pretty unsophisticated when it came to movies.

This was during a time when my Zen practice had become very difficult. It was my can't-get-no-satisfaction phase, and all sorts of memories and fears were coming up in my meditation. Over and over, I relived past dramas and projected them into the future, rehearsing how I wanted to be different. The stillness and joy I'd experienced my first few months of Zen practice had vanished. I seemed to have no control over the images that cycled through my mind, on and off the cushion.

"I like them all," was a teaching that I didn't recognize until much later. Even though I didn't understand the significance of those four words at the time, they stayed with me. Suzuki wasn't judging the movies he saw. He wasn't comparing them to the artsy films playing at North Beach. He was simply present, attentive, and engaged. This was his way.

Today, people say that Suzuki Roshi was a great enlightened being, but I don't know about that. He lived lightly, joyfully. That is what I remember most about him. It's what drew me to him and continues to draw me to him, though now he lives only in my heart.

"I like them all" was a footprint along my path, one that disappeared and reappeared, over and over, until I finally got it. I realized that I could be present and attentive to the movies inside my head without getting caught up in which ones were good and which were bad.

I think this is a challenge that most of us face. We create movies in our heads to try to make sense of the world and of what's happening around us. But these movies are based on our memories of past experiences, and if they're so dense we can't see beyond them, they tether us continually to the past.

We can learn something about ourselves if we look closely at these movies and recognize their genres and themes. When we're fearful, our movies may be tension-filled dramas. When moody or anxious, gloomy melodramas. For many people, ghost stories are a favorite genre. Here's one of mine:

In the mid-sixties, there weren't many of us meditators, so I got to hang out with Suzuki as much as I wanted. Then we purchased Tassajara Zen Mountain Monastery, and more and more people came to practice with him. Things began to change.

I had a friend whom I'll call Louise. She was a serious Zen student, and I appreciated her sincerity. But after a while it seemed that she was dominating Suzuki's time and I began to appreciate her less and less. Whenever I saw her, I was overwhelmed with jealousy and confusion.

Finally, I realized what was going on. In this situation Louise was like my sister, and I was jealous of my sister my whole life because my dad seemed to give her more time and attention than me. I became aware that the movie I'd created so many years ago was now playing out even here in this calm, monastic setting, dedicated to the cultivation of stillness, compassion, and deep inner joy. I was trying my best to live in today—but memory ghosts swirled around me, separating me from what was actually going on. I felt isolated even while surrounded by kind and caring people.

This is the human situation: We often see others through our prior experiences and expectations. We are so mesmerized by these ghostly images that we don't really encounter each other. Memory ghosts can be so dense and murky that we can't see through them, forming a protective shell that makes us feel disconnected from life.

Memory ghosts sometimes signal a deep hurt or disappointment that needs to be attended to and released. So we have to pay attention to the types of movies that cycle through our minds. If we learn to see them clearly without judgment or criticism and without getting caught up in them, they can serve a deeper purpose, becoming an inner resource that nourishes our aspiration and offers insight and emotional release.

Throughout this book, I'll offer hints and techniques to guide you along, but in the end we learn how to do this deep inner work by doing it. If you stay with it, at some point you will begin to disidentify with your movies and experience an inner openness that allows you to remain receptive to life. Eventually, you'll learn to recognize responses that sustain this openness. But first, you'll have to see clearly those responses that close you down.

CAUGHT IN A SELF-CENTERED DREAM

We know so many things but we don't know ourselves.

—MEISTER ECKHART

I'd like to share a story about a woman I'll call Alice. Alice had a beautiful daughter that she was proud of. She was very involved in her daughter's life, and she considered herself to be a good mother, but when her daughter went to college and had a psychotic break, everything changed. Alice felt responsible. This was the early seventies, a time when many people believed that mental illness was inherited from the mother. So now, in Alice's mind, she was a bad mother. To escape her guilt, she began to drink heavily.

She went into therapy that lasted for several years, during which time she learned that her daughter's schizophrenia had nothing to do with her. Alice became a mental health advocate, because she now felt that she was a good person with something meaningful to contribute.

Then Alice's youngest son got kicked out of college for using drugs, and her husband left her for her best friend. Now Alice felt that she was a terrible mother, a terrible wife, and even a terrible human being.

Soon thereafter, her daughter with schizophrenia gave birth to an adorable baby that they parented together, and Alice became a happy, fulfilled mother and grandmother. A few years later, however, her daughter went off her meds, had paranoid delusions, and ran off with the child. Who did Alice think she was then?

Like Alice, many people wander through life experiencing a series of changing roles, like actors in a succession of movies. Who are we in the midst of all these roles? Are we our ideas? Are we our thoughts, our concerns, our movies? Or are we the extended feelings, the moods, the instinctual urges that underlie the movie-making world that we live in?

Meditation is about seeing the multiplicity of roles we identify with, and the way these roles continuously arise and vanish. If we hold them lightly, the roles remain transparent, allowing us to see and appreciate their ever-changing nature.

As Alice's story shows, we identify with certain components of our experience, tie these components together, and call this string of events our *self.* This seems to be the nature of our movie-making mind. These mental movies have the capacity to either diminish or enrich our lives.

Buddha taught that what we experience as continuity arises from a continuous flow of activity, rather than a solid, unchanging self. Alice's story points to the key to understanding the wisdom of this chapter.

We begin to experience freedom from our habituated way of experiencing the world as we learn to see the self as a process rather than a solid being moving through time. For most of us, however, freedom from our fear-based way of thinking does not come easily.

In the thick of the forest is where you will find your freedom.

—BUDDHA

We never know when we're going to find ourselves in the thick of the forest. For my friend Sydney, a long-time meditator, the discovery of freedom came through a major stroke that left her unable to speak. When I went to see her, she used a writing pad to communicate. Her hand shook uncontrollably as she wrote, "I'm okay. Learned not this face. Learned not this body." When I looked at her, her eyes were suffused with loving acceptance.

Sydney found peace, even tranquility, after her stroke because she had sustained a regular meditation practice for many years. Even a practice of only twenty minutes a day can help you hold your movie-making response lightly.

To really penetrate the movies and follow them all the way in so as to see the patterns that produce them, however, requires more. That's why we have Zen retreats that last from three days to a week or even longer.

A few years ago, during a long retreat, a student came to see me for a private meeting. She said, "I think it's going well because my mind has gotten very quiet. But it's kind of scary. Who will I be if I lose myself? How will I function in the world?" As she spoke she churned up more and more doubt until finally she exclaimed, "I think I should go home now."

This frequently happens in Zen retreats. When you finally experience some stillness, these questions become relevant. How do you identify with non-being? There's nothing there to identify with. It can be disconcerting at first. But it's right here, in the thick of the forest, that we discover a wonderful freedom that our movie-making mind cannot touch.

I encouraged the retreat participant to stay with her anxiety and ride it out. She agreed to give it try. When she came to see me a couple of days later, her mood was quite different. She spoke of the stillness and peacefulness she was experiencing. "When the bell rang to end a meditation session, my body rose on its own. My body knows what to do."

Whatever you experience in meditation becomes your teacher if you just stay with it. Even asthma can be your teacher, as my friend Eleanor discovered. Eleanor was planning a long retreat with Katagiri Roshi, then the guiding teacher of Minnesota Zen Meditation Center. She was worried about doing the retreat because she had to use an inhaler frequently. That meant she would have to use it during meditation, but she was clinging to her idea that she should not move during meditation.

Katagiri Roshi encouraged her to do the retreat. He counseled her to be with the stress in her throat if she could and to use her inhaler whenever she needed to. "Use the stress in your throat as the object of your meditation," he said.

Eleanor began the retreat knowing that she could use her inhaler any time. But as the retreat went on, she was able to relax into the stress in her throat more and more. She stayed for the entire seven-day retreat. By the end, she noticed that her throat muscles had relaxed and her breath was not so shallow.

By being with it rather than trying to avoid or escape it, asthma became Eleanor's thick of the forest. It became a place of freedom where before there was only limitation.

Being human can feel like being trapped—trapped in a body that demands and bullies, a mind that ridicules and spins out over every little thing, a dangerous and confounding world. But is it really that way? The next three chapters will take you into the darkest forest, to the very places where we feel most lost and most vulnerable. But you'll have a guide and a flashlight. All you need to bring is an open mind and a willing heart. The last section of each chapter, Doing the Work, is where your eyes begin to adjust to the dark, and your own insight becomes your guide.

CORE MEDITATION PRACTICE FOR CALMING AND CENTERING

If you're meditating at home, it's important to designate a certain place for your practice. It can also help to create a bit of ritual that signals to your brain your intention to meditate. You might begin by closing the blinds or curtains, dimming the lights, lighting a candle, or perhaps burning a bit of incense. Take each step with your full attention. Feel the floor against your feet and the feel of the match or lighter as you light the candle; notice how the flame flares up and the smoke curls and spirals. When these tasks are performed with attentiveness, always in the same order, and with one-pointed focus, they become a calming and centering ritual. Your mind will start to settle down before you even begin the meditation.

During meditation, when your mind becomes distracted from your breath (and it will, over and over), try to notice the distraction and then return without comment or reactivity. When some emotional reactivity does bubble up, say frustration or irritation, focus on the bodily sensations of frustration or irritation rather than your thoughts. Stay with the sensations until they dissolve and then return to the object of focus. Don't try to suppress your thoughts. The point is to become aware of your thought patterns by noticing the arising of a pattern without getting caught up in it. That's why we stay focused on the breath, using it as an anchor so we can see our patterns without reinforcing them.

Start by taking a few deep breaths and notice where in your body you feel your breath most prominently. It may be in your nostrils, or as your breath moves down your throat, or in the rise and fall of your chest or belly. Just rest your focus in that area and then allow your breath to return to its natural rhythm, without trying to control it. If your breath is shallow and quick, let it be shallow and quick; if it's slow and deep, let it be slow and deep. Feel the openness that allows the breath to come and go on its own, without hindrance. Bring that same non-attached openness to whatever arises in your mind.

Allowing your breath, thoughts, emotions, and sensations to arise and then dissolve on their own is one of the most difficult things for a human being to do. The specific nature of the difficulty reveals something about our own patterns of reactivity. Is it difficult to let your breath be, without controlling or judging? Do you get agitated or angry when you catch your mind wandering off? You can start to free yourself from your inner control freak by simply observing the rhythm of your own breath without interfering and then extending that gentle attentiveness to your thoughts and emotions as they arise.

As we follow the natural rhythm of our breath, we begin to discover in an experiential way that our thoughts, sensations, and emotions come and go as naturally as the breath if we do not cling to them or try to avoid them. Of course emotions are more viscous and slow-moving than breath, but they come and go nevertheless, because this is the natural rhythm of life. It is only our fear that we'll be overwhelmed by our emotions or do something stupid that makes us feel out of balance or out of sync with reality. Meditation gives us the opportunity to get to know our emotions in an intimate way so we're comfortable with them. Even the strong emotions that we try so hard to avoid become fresh new avenues of insight and deepen our capacity for compassion.

DOING THE WORK

1. Think for a moment about a personal narrative—a mental movie—that you play over and over in your mind. As an antidote, imagine the unfolding of an opposite story. See if you can find a memory that affirms this new story line. Or you may bring to mind a memory that supports the old story line—and open yourself up to a new interpretation.

2. Recall a time when you found yourself in the thick of the forest. What did this experience teach you about yourself?

TWO

The Trance of
Unworthiness

ONCE THE DALAI LAMA was asked by an American about how to deal with self-hatred. The question startled him. He turned to his interpreter for an explanation, but the more his interpreter tried to explain the phenomenon of self-hatred, the more confused the Dalai Lama became. Finally, he turned back to the questioner and said, "Self-hatred. What is that?"

In the ensuing discussion, the Dalai Lama asked for a show of hands of those who had experienced self-hatred. Viewing all the raised hands, he concluded, "I thought I had a very good acquaintance with the mind, but now I feel quite ignorant. I find this very, very strange."

For many in the United States and possibly most Western cultures, feelings of unworthiness like those that puzzled the Dalai Lama are pervasive. In chapter one, we discussed how we are enticed into a self-centered dream, hypnotized by the movies we make. In this chapter, we'll look at the trance-like state we get caught in when our original nature is veiled by feelings of guilt, shame, remorse, anguish, and resentment. We may even feel as if we're sleepwalking through life.

Healing happens naturally as we penetrate these trance-inducing veils with mindful attention. We start by seeing clearly the thought patterns that cause us so much pain. We have to see how these patterns are triggered, how they arise, and how they dissolve. In this chapter, we'll begin to understand how so many of our habituated responses are based on cognitive misperceptions, conditioned emotional reactivity, and coping mechanisms that have outlived their usefulness.

The primary trance-inducing veil is fear. When we're stuck in fear-based thinking, we are driven by a need to protect ourselves and may act out in inappropriate and destructive ways. The more we do this, the deeper our trance of unworthiness becomes.

When we use objects like food or intoxicants, or engage in activities like shopping or gambling or even worshipping to avoid feeling the sensation of fear, fear acts like a veil. We may even use spiritual objects like altars. Maybe you have an altar in every corner of your house. Well, that's fine if they are meant to remind you that everyday life is the place of enlightenment. But if you're thinking that the spiritual is different from the mundane, that the calmness of a spiritual life is different from the unruly surf of this great oceanic life, and if you cling to the presence of your altars as a way to escape the fear-inducing realities of the world, then you are caught in a movie about living a spiritual life. In real life, it is the nature of the ocean to create surf. Being afraid of the surf helps to induce a trance that can trap us.

A second trance-inducing veil is anger. Anger is a big wave. We often get bowled over by anger arising from insecurity and from the need to succeed, to dominate, and to feel loved and valued.

A historical example of the destructive power of anger is Adolf Hitler. He was charismatic and smart, but the primary emotion he tapped into was anger.

It's important to recognize the power of our emotions. Emotions tend to drive our lives. The word *drive* in this context might sound negative, but it can also be positive. Look at Barack Obama. He is charismatic and smart. He can run different narratives simultaneously: philosophical ones, psychological ones, political ones—but it's the depth of his hope, courage, joy, and love that sustains him. Emotions drive Obama's life in a positive way.

Another example of someone who understood the power of emotions was Suzuki Roshi. I often hear people say that Suzuki was deeply enlightened. But Suzuki himself said, "There are no enlightened people, only enlightened activity." He manifested enlightenment in the way he lived his life. He radiated love, but he never talked about love. He was in the United States for only twelve years before he died. But look at what he accomplished for the dharma in those twelve years. He rooted Soto Zen Buddhism in America—an amazing feat.

A third trance-inducing veil is anxiety. When I began my Zen practice, my father was concerned about what I was doing with my life. He said, "Tim, I just want you to know that I think what you are pursuing is not possible. A lot of people are into this religious stuff because they think they can get some enduring peace of mind. But I've been around for a long time, and there's no such thing. I hope you don't waste your life!"

At a young age, I recognized how much my father suffered from anxiety about social acceptance and money, even though he was quite successful. He suffered from deeply ingrained feelings of insecurity. Achievement became his avoidance strategy. In the United States, avoidance is a common coping mechanism. But no matter how much my father achieved, the underlying fear that he was not good enough remained and his coping mechanism drove him to seek more and more success. Avoidance didn't bring him the freedom from anxiety that he sought.

The suffering I saw in my dad was one of the reasons I was drawn to the counterculture. While my father sought solace within the mainstream social and economic system—what we young rebels called "the establishment"—I *blamed* the establishment. Blaming the establishment became *my* avoidance strategy. It was a coping mechanism I would have to rethink after I finished college and became a social worker, a vocation that is funded and maintained by the establishment.

So far, I've discussed three trance-inducing veils. Now we'll delve more deeply into each of these common afflictions. Then we'll focus on three qualities that allow us to live more skillfully, without withdrawing from or indulging in the turbulent energies of fear, anger, and anxiety.

SUSTAINING THE TRANCE THROUGH FEAR, ANGER, AND ANXIETY

Fear. First, it's important to recognize that fear-based thinking is evolutionary. It is called the "negativity bias," and scientists believe it originated as an adaptive mechanism to help human beings survive. Imagine that one of our early ancestors saw rustling in tall grasses. If his instincts consistently told him it was a tiger, rather than a rabbit, his risk of extinction decreased. In these circumstances, fear saved lives.

Today in the developed countries of the world we generally do not live in life-threatening situations, but the fear response still gets activated. And when our thoughts are fear-based, we tend to be either overtly or passively aggressive, conflict-avoidant, or frozen by indecision.

We like going to movies that keep us on the edge of our seats. All we have to do is suspend our disbelief and go for a thrilling ride. Along the way, we experience happiness, sadness, anger, fear, anxiety, bewilderment, agitation; emotions and mental states pass through our body like waves through the ocean.

Poet and philosopher Samuel Taylor Coleridge, who coined the phrase "suspension of disbelief" in 1817, said that if a writer could infuse a story with a "human interest and a semblance of truth," readers would make a semiconscious decision to put aside their disbelief and accept the premise for the duration of the story. This can be a way of deepening our aesthetic response to a work of art. Unfortunately, we often make the same semiconscious decision to suspend our disbelief when watching the movies we create in our mind—despite the fact that these personal movies are mostly divorced from reality.

The inner movies I hear about the most as a Zen teacher have some common themes: "I'm not good enough to calm my mind. I'm not disciplined enough. My mind is too chaotic and my emotions are too sticky."

What is going on when people think they can't meditate?

During meditation, while our awareness is focused on the breath, our fear-based patterns begin to reveal themselves. When discomfort arises in the form of physical or emotional pain, we usually respond in one of three ways: we fight it, becoming agitated and irritable; we try to escape the discomfort through fantasy and then feel guilty or ashamed that we are wasting our time in meditation; or we freeze up like a stone, holding our mind in a state of rigid, unfeeling blankness.

Here in Minnesota, where I now live and teach, we tend to emphasize the first and third reactions—flight or freeze—when it comes to our relationships with others. "Minnesota nice" can be a superficial way of dealing with people that hides emotions and fosters mistrust. In other parts of the country, New York City for instance, people tend toward the fight response: social encounters may quickly devolve into verbal skirmishes.

It is possible to respond skillfully to fear-based thinking, to meet it with both honesty and kindness. Without honesty, kindness may devolve into sentimentality or complacency. Without kindness, honesty may devolve into self-loathing or righteous condemnation of others. The combination of honesty and kindness characterizes the kind of enlightened activity that I witnessed in Suzuki Roshi.

When you're caught in a scary movie, being honest and kind isn't usually your first thought. Even if you're not caught in a movie—even if you're experiencing life directly—when you're all churned up inside being honest and kind is not easy. It takes courage, commitment, and the willingness to experience the sensations associated with negative emotions. With practice, enlightened activity can become your default response, even in the presence of fear.

Anger. Anger is addictive because it has so much power. People around us pay attention when we become angry. But often we don't realize how dominating anger is. It can control our lives.

On September 11, 2001, planes crashed into the World Trade Center in New York City. We Americans were angry. The leaders of our government were angry, especially the trio of President George W. Bush, Vice President Dick Cheney, and Secretary of Defense Donald Rumsfeld. It's natural to be angry when you've been attacked. But what did they do with it? Did they deny their anger? Did they repress their anger? What did they do with their anger?

They magnified and generalized. They revved up their anger, and they revved up the anger of the country. Then they aimed it at several countries and at millions of people in the Middle East. The results were destructive and irrational. Years later we are still asking ourselves, why did we invade and occupy Iraq, a country that had nothing to do with the bombing of the World Trade Center?

One reason anger is so powerful is that it is a mechanism of survival. We need it. But how do we work with it so it doesn't become a weapon of destruction?

First of all, we have to believe that anger can be purified of its toxic content and channeled in wholesome and creative ways. Anger provides information. We know that physical pain should not be ignored; it is informing us of a problem that needs our attention. Likewise, anger informs you that your mind and heart are in pain. So anger is not a problem—it is a messenger.

The key is to bring our strong emotions like anger into view without fueling them with our stories. In meditation, we learn to observe the arising of a strong emotion, to feel its intensity and notice where in our body it is held, and to begin to see the reactive patterns that occur. We see how we magnify and generalize by making stories out of our feelings. We weave a web around the emotion and then get caught in it, often catching others as well.

However, we can learn to work with the energy of anger and let go of the content. In my first book, *Nothing Holy about It*, I described my brother's suicide and the anger I had to cope with. Eventually I was able to channel its energy into creating programs that help people who suffer from depression, as my brother had.

We have the capacity to work with our anger skillfully, without generalizing or magnifying. It's all about letting go of the content, and we learn how to let go by doing it over and over in meditation. As you work with anger in this way, you develop the capacity to tolerate, and even appreciate, its chaotic energy.

Anger arises for a reason from your karmic past. You can cultivate a compassionate relationship with it that deepens your understanding of the human condition and deepens your capacity for intimacy with others.

Anxiety. The seeds of anxiety that I inherited from my father and from my own karmic past will always be with me, waiting to be watered.

A few years ago, I injured my back. I was in a lot of pain, especially at night. I was in my mid-sixties and had never previously experienced much bodily pain. But now a pattern developed in which I woke up throughout the night in pain.

After a while, I became anxious about going to bed. What were my choices? I could watch TV instead of lying down. Or I could take a pain pill. But I wasn't in pain yet; I was just anxious about the possibility of pain. Of course, I could take the pill anyway in anticipation of the pain to come.

Neither of my two choices aligned with the path to freedom. If I clung to my anxiety about the pain and stayed up until three in the morning watching TV in order to avoid going to bed, then I would *have* to take a pain pill anyway, so I could allow myself to fall asleep. Often our coping mechanisms create even bigger problems for us.

Thankfully, I had a third option: to lie down, breathe, and pay attention to the ebb and flow of sensations in my body. The Zen path is to learn to tolerate our aches and pains without suffering so much from them. We learn it by doing it, by allowing our kind awareness to flow *with* the pain rather than rebelling against it or trying to escape it. When we can do this, we don't make big things out of small things. Moreover, if we can manage our physical pain in this way, we can do the same with our emotional pain as well.

Another way we make big things out of little things is by layering other reactive emotions on top of anxiety and fear—for example, when we experience shame and embarrassment about having anxiety and fear.

I'm the guiding teacher at Minnesota Zen Meditation Center. What will people think if they know I have anxiety about going to sleep at night? Am I worthy of being a Zen teacher? Projecting our anxiety inward and making up stories about it is a behavior pattern that increases and sustains our feelings of unworthiness.

We also project our feelings of unworthiness outward. I met a man recently who had moved to Minnesota from another state. He said he had been going to a Zen center there but he quit because the teacher didn't like him. I asked whether he'd discussed the problem with the teacher.

"Oh no," he said. "I didn't want to do that."

"How do you know he didn't like you?" I asked.

"Because he was always frowning when he looked at me."

"Was he frowning or just being serious?"

"Well, it seemed like he was frowning. I felt like there was no room for me there."

But he didn't check it out. He was just projecting, and his projections became his reality. We do that all the time, and it causes so much pain and confusion.

Anxiety in itself isn't necessarily destructive. Like anger, anxiety has an important function in our life. It tells us something about our environment and ourselves. My anxiety helps me to see and understand my patterns and fears. I can see how I often respond to discomfort, embarrassment, or shame by closing down to unpleasant sensations, instead of allowing the sensations to come and go like waves in the ocean.

LIVING SKILLFULLY THROUGH OPENNESS, NONJUDGMENTAL AWARENESS, AND KINDNESS

All that we are is based on our thoughts. If you act on a wise thought, happiness follows you like a shadow that never leaves you. If you act on an unwise thought, unhappiness follows you like a shadow that never leaves you.

—BUDDHA

Fear-based thinking is instinctual, but human beings are not limited to instinct. Our thoughts emanate from our beliefs and concepts about the world. Meditation expands our awareness; a spaciousness opens up that often defies our small egoic ideas about how things are. When our heart and mind are open, we begin to experience what interconnectedness and interdependence are all about. Our skin doesn't just divide us; it also connects us to all beings. Here in Minnesota, our northern boundary joins us to Canada. As human beings, our skin joins us to our surroundings in a manner that can be deeply satisfying. With a little thought it becomes obvious that we feel the heat of the sun through our skin, or the cold of a snowflake, or the touch of another person. Zen is about compelling people to think deeply.

While an intellectual understanding of interconnectedness is a good place to begin, it is not enough to be transformative. We have to get it inside us, in our body, all the way down to the marrow. We have to know it in a visceral way. Otherwise, it's just another mental construct, a movie where the hero is a wise sage.

So how do we go from a mental understanding to an embodied understanding? Embodiment is not about changing who we are—but that doesn't mean it doesn't involve change.

When I was living at Tassajara Zen Mountain Monastery, certain days were designated as free days, on which we could do whatever we wanted. On one of these free days, I met with Suzuki to grumble about the way things were going. For one thing, we had to wear robes even though we weren't ordained, and robes were difficult for me. Mine were always higgledy-piggledy, and I stepped on them whenever I stood up from the cushion.

Another problem was the introduction of a ritualized meal service called *oryoki*. It involved nested bowls wrapped and tied in several layers of linen and a series of meal chants to memorize. The meal unfolded in orchestrated stages. It was quite beautiful, but I wasn't good at ritual, so I was pissing and moaning because I felt awkward and clumsy.

Suzuki responding by saying, "You are perfect just as you are."

Perfect just as I am? What a relief! I didn't have to worry about my robes or mastering the traditional monastic meal service because I was perfect as I was. So I spent the rest of my free day hiking along the streams and hills above Tassajara.

Suzuki recognized that I was becoming fixated on ideas about how I should be and how my practice should be. Through his kindness, I was able to relax into what was happening in my practice, and I experienced some openness. When we're open, we're resilient. Only then can practice continue.

However, Suzuki's lesson for me that day was not finished. When I came back to my little cabin that afternoon, he motioned me over. I immediately started telling him about my day, how wonderful it was.

He listened patiently. Then he said, "But Tim, you could use a little improvement in the way you take care of things."

"You are perfect as you are, but you can use a little improvement," has become one of Suzuki Roshi's best-known quotations. It exemplifies his skillfulness as a teacher. If you just go with the first part—*you're perfect as you are*—you're probably flaking out on your commitments. If you just go with the second part—*you could use a little improvement*—you're probably beating yourself up around some idea of who you should be. You need both.

The openness, nonjudgmental awareness, and kindness that Suzuki embodied are aspects of our original nature. These qualities arise naturally when the mind becomes still through regular meditation. Here, then, is the key for dissolving the trance of unworthiness.

> KEY #2: Meditation is the antidote
> for feelings of unworthiness.

In the heat of the moment, however, openness, nonjudgmental awareness, and kindness can be difficult to open up to.

My wife, Linda, and I have two cats that are pretty old. Once, when Linda was out of town, one of the cats started peeing on everything. She peed on the floor, on the bath mat, on our Oriental rug. I put my pajamas on the floor just for a few minutes, and she peed on them. I felt like throwing her outside.

For a moment, I couldn't imagine how to deal with my anger. But all I had to do was pet her and feel the connectedness between my hand and her fur, and I was able to see and appreciate her just as she was, rather than comparing her to the cat she used to be. My anger dissolved, my body relaxed, and a deep appreciation for this continuously unfolding life returned.

SURFING THE GREAT OCEAN OF LIFE

When I was a teenager in Northern California, my friend Jerry and I would go to Santa Cruz after school to surf. Surfing was pretty big in Southern California where the water was warm, but had not yet become popular in Santa Cruz. Jerry and I were usually the only ones there, surfing the cold water with no wet suits. Jerry had a surfboard and I bodysurfed. When the really big waves came, they often knocked me over and took me under.

The ocean is a good metaphor for our interconnected life. With a regular meditation practice, we can learn to surf life's waves, but chances are good that we will sometimes be overpowered by them for a while.

A technique like following your breath is a great surfboard for riding these waves. But when the surf is up and you're being submerged in wave after wave of fear, anger, and anxiety, you may need a more specialized surfboard, possibly adding counting your breath, repeating a mantra or phrase that is meaningful to you, or doing walking meditation rather than simply sitting still.

Sometimes Jerry and I felt as if we were wasting our time trying to surf—we were just getting knocked over by one wave after another. Days and sometimes even weeks went by when we weren't making any progress at all—very discouraging. Life can be like that, but with a regular meditation practice, you learn to experience each wave not as an obstacle to your real life but *as* your real life. Eventually you may learn to enjoy the surf directly, with no board at all, experiencing the joy of being fully immersed in the water, regardless of its turbulent energies.

Each wave has its own unique nature. It also has the nature of the entire ocean, because a wave is not separate from the ocean. You learn to be patient when you're riding the energy of the entire ocean. Jerry and I surfed on calm days and on stormy days. Surfing on stormy days isn't easy, but the storm is never separate from the calmness down below.

Even so, for every thrilling swell that lifts you upward toward the sky, there is a trough that can send you reeling into the darkest depths. Troughs are part of the ocean, too. When you're in a deep trough, you can't go forward and you can't retreat. Nor can you predict what will come next, because you can't see beyond the trough. In the troughs, you learn to trust, to have courage, and to be patient—qualities that come naturally if you're committed to surfing the entire ocean.

Another quality that comes naturally as you learn to surf is renunciation. Jerry and I had to practice renunciation every day. Because we wanted to surf in the afternoons, we renounced driving our souped-up cars up and down the street in front of Palo Alto High after school where everyone could see us. Jerry renounced smoking so he could keep his lungs in good shape to handle the strong currents and mammoth waves. We even had to renounce hanging out with girls in the afternoons. It wasn't easy to give up these things that we liked, but we had fallen in love with surfing, so we did it.

Renunciation is a matter of putting aside our immediate desires just a little bit so we can stay focused on something bigger. As Jerry and I waited in the water, watching the horizon for a wave big enough to carry us all the way in to shore, we were often tempted to take whatever wave came along. Resisting that temptation was another form of renunciation. Training in renunciation involves seeing our immediate desires as they arise without indulging them.

If you indulge a desire, what happens next? Another desire arises. And another and another. The faster you indulge your desires, the faster they come. You'll never learn to surf if you are distracted by the small waves that constantly lap at your surfboard.

After a while, the small steady waves of desire no longer distract you. Eventually, even the surfboard begins to dissolve because you no longer need it. Suddenly, you realize that you are right there in the surf with no gap, no separation between you and the waves, completely immersed in the ocean.

Wave by wave is how we stay engaged with life. It is the only way to experience the immediacy and vigor that real life offers. Sure, it's raw. But we don't need to protect ourselves from the moods and nuances of life's great ocean. We can stay right with it, in placid times and in turbulent times. Life is always offering us the energy and vitality we need—just let the salt water seep into your pores.

I'll end this chapter with an untitled poem written in the thirteenth century by Zen master Dogen, which I've adapted slightly. To understand this poem, it's important to know that the moon is a metaphor for wisdom and that birds are a metaphor for thoughts. Dogen writes about being entranced by thoughts of judgment and ridicule: this is worthy; that is not. Then, a great insight arises.

> All my life
> True and false,
> Right and wrong
> Are entangled.
> Playing with the moon
> Ridiculing the wind
> Listening to the birds
> Many years wasted.
> Seeing the ocean
> White with surf,
> This year
> I suddenly realized
> Surf makes the ocean.

Can you learn to surf the chaos and uncertainty that real life includes without falling into a trance of unworthiness? You can. A surfer is powerless to change the towering wave rushing toward her. But she doesn't want to change it. She wants to surf it and she learns to feel safe in the immense ocean of being even when she falls. She confidently gets right back up to meet the next wave.

A MEDITATION FOR DISSOLVING FEELINGS OF UNWORTHINESS

The following meditation will help you develop the capacity to be nonjudgmental and kind toward yourself and others. We can all develop the ability to discover and transmit pure, unconditioned love, the natural manifestation of each wave's undividedness from the huge ocean.

We begin with ourselves. Then we extend kindness to our loved ones, our friends and acquaintances, and then to those with whom we have difficulty. There may be certain people you are not ready to extend kindness toward. Don't push yourself. At some point, you may be surprised to experience an expansive awareness that easily includes everyone.

Begin with the core meditation for calming and centering (pages 14–16). When you're ready, repeat the phrases below slowly. Pause after each line to arouse and nurture the felt-sense associated with the words so your entire being is fully engaged and participating.

May I feel safe and protected.
May I feel free of mental suffering and distress.
May I feel healthy and strong.
May I live in this world happily, peacefully, joyfully, and
    with ease.

Repeat the phrase until you feel a sense of warmth throughout your body. When you're ready, think of a person who is close to you, for whom it takes no effort to feel warmth and kindness toward. Repeat the phrases for this person: "May she or he feel safe and protected . . ."

After you have steeped yourself in feelings of tenderness for this person, move on to someone who is more neutral in your life, a friend or colleague. Continue to steep yourself in tender and caring feelings.

Now turn to someone for whom you harbor hostile feelings and resentments. Repeat the phrases for this person. If you have difficulty doing this, you can say, "To the best of my ability, I wish that you feel safe and protected . . ." If you begin to feel ill will toward this person, return to a loved one and allow the tenderness to arise again. Then return to this person.

Rather than attempting to dissolve hostile feelings, surround them with tenderness. These hostile feelings point out your own suffering. Offer your compassion as you would to any other being who is suffering. Allow compassion to penetrate the isolated feelings of hostility. Hold both at the same time and notice what happens.

When you're ready, use the phrases to extend the feelings of tenderness to everyone around the world. No one is excluded. This expanded consciousness absorbs and transforms our feelings of unworthiness. Self-hatred cannot exist here. Healing arises when we create the conditions for healing to arise. This is Buddha's most fundamental teaching. You can trust it.

You may end this session by returning for five or ten minutes to the core meditation for calming and centering (pages 14–16).

DOING THE WORK

The point of this chapter has been to demystify our emotional reactivity so we can live with buoyancy and skillfulness, even during emotional storms. The following exercises are designed to help you see your emotional patterns and practice staying with them without acting them out until they dissolve on their own.

1. For the next week, notice what category of thought and/or behavior you most frequently engage in when afraid or anxious:

fight, flight, or freeze. After identifying your predominant pattern, when it next arises, pause and breathe deeply for two or three minutes into and around the desire to fight, flee, or freeze. Notice what happens each time.

2. Notice one opinion or belief that you hold strongly. Consciously interact with someone who has a radically different belief than yours, listening to them very carefully and empathetically so you can get a sense of why that belief is so important to them. Look into your own thought patterns to discover why your belief is so important to you.

3. Notice each time you start putting yourself down. Take three deep breaths and then find the kindness within yourself that you might extend to a sick child. Consciously expand it until it suffuses your entire body and mind. Steep yourself in this kindness for as long as you can. When it fades, notice whether you feel lighter and more at peace with yourself. Consider the possibility that this tenderness is more authentic than the harshness you experience when you engage in thoughts of unworthiness.

THREE

Sex

L OOKING AROUND TODAY, it's hard to believe that
American culture has a puritanical heritage. In
the 1940s and 50s, we were a shut-down and repressed society.
Young boys never saw a female breast. Even infants never saw their
mother's breast, because Americans believed research showed that
bottle-fed babies were healthier than breast-fed babies. But this
research was driven by corporate America, by male-dominated
science, and perhaps by the underlying idea that female breasts
were indecent.

Now look at what's going on. We reacted to the puritanism of
the fifties by going to the other extreme. America has become a
hyper-sexualized society. It's easy to see why: we are a consumer
culture, after all, and sex sells. But the pendulum has swung so
far that even corporate America is feeling the heat: employees
watching porn at work have become a major problem.

So how do we respond to our human tendency to bounce
back and forth between puritanism and self-indulgence? First,

it's important to realize that the bounce is fear-based. It is driven by insecurity. We want something we can count on, so what do we do? We make rules about right and wrong, and these rules make us feel secure, because they clarify our worldview. But then we right-and-wrong each other to death, clinging to narrow-minded rules that make us feel superior to others. Rules like these spare us the burden of having to recognize and integrate the experiences of others into our worldview. Too often, obedience replaces compassion. It even happens in spiritual communities where compassion is supposed to be a core value.

There's a story about two disciples who got into an argument about the true spiritual path. The first said, "The path is built on effort and energy. You must pray, live diligently, and devote yourself completely according to the law."

The second disciple countered, "It's not effort at all. That is only based on ego. It's pure surrender. The true way is to let go of all things and to live the teaching."

The two disciples went to see the rabbi. He listened as the first disciple praised the path of wholehearted effort. "Isn't this the true path?" he asked.

"You're right," the rabbi replied.

The second disciple protested. He eloquently described the path of surrender and then asked, "Is this not the true path?"

"You're right," said the rabbi.

A third student who'd overheard the discussion interjected, "But Rabbi, they can't both be right."

"You're right, too."

The point of the story is that in wholeness, all of our imperfections and flaws are included. Accepting what is alleviates feelings of alienation and separation that come from bouncing between indulgence and deprivation.

Buddha offered five precepts that help us be more like the rabbi. Buddhist precepts aren't rules. Buddha referred to them as gifts. They point to a way of living from which happiness arises naturally without being dependent on external conditions.

A close examination of these precepts is beyond the scope of this chapter, so I'll just offer a brief overview. The first two foster respectfulness for life and the property of others. The third concerns sexuality; the fourth, interpersonal relationships. The fifth concerns intoxicants, meaning anything that impedes clear thinking, which includes intoxicating fantasies and even religious intoxication.

In this chapter, we are mostly concerned with the third precept—acting responsibly in matters of sexuality. This precept is about not objectifying others. It concerns intimacy rather than morality. It concerns our attitude toward sex rather than the act of sex itself.

The precepts are about actualizing interconnectedness in everyday life. It sounds complicated, but nothing is more simple or straightforward. Kindness is a natural and spontaneous response when our heart and mind are undivided. When heart and mind are one, rules are not necessary; in fact, rules can even impede our natural intimacy with all beings. I think everyone prefers relationships that are authentic, not ones that are regulated by rules of conduct.

The following Taoist poem, translated by Jonathan Star, beautifully illuminates the difference between adherence to rules and authentic virtue, which arises naturally from what Buddha called *bodhicitta*, meaning "heart-mind."

The highest virtue is to act without a sense of self
The highest kindness is to give without condition
The highest justice is to see without preference

When Tao is lost one must learn the rules of virtue
When virtue is lost, the rules of kindness
When kindness is lost, the rules of justice
When justice is lost, the rules of conduct

—TAO TE CHING

The qualities of heart-mind include openness, honesty, and compassion. Even with regular meditation, it isn't always easy to actualize a united heart and mind. When the surf is up, and we feel wounded, fearful, and confused, rules can save us from hurting others and we can rely on them until stability returns. That reliance drops away naturally as we reconnect with our great oceanic life, where all the waves in the ocean continuously intermingle.

ZEN AND SEXUALITY

In the time of Buddha, living the life of a monk required a lot of energy. Except during the rainy seasons, monks traveled by foot from place to place, eating only what was offered to them, so conserving energy was important. Celibacy was emphasized because it was practical on many levels, as one might imagine.

From a Zen point of view, sex is not immoral or sinful, but it is a powerful force—so much so that it can distract us from our commitment to meditation. If you want to wake up to your true interdependent nature, your commitment to practice has to permeate your life. As long as an active sex life doesn't interfere with that commitment, sex is not condemned.

Since Zen does not dictate a moral code of conduct, we don't differentiate between reproductive and recreational sex. On college campuses today, "hooking up" is as common as dating. Well, that's fine, as long as there is a mutual understanding and respectfulness.

I don't think a spiritual practice is healthy if it doesn't accept the intrinsic pleasure of sex. If we can accept the intrinsic pleasure of the sun's warmth, the sound of rain, a good meal, or the ecstasy of an enlightenment experience—then why not the pleasure of sex? Living a Zen life is about letting go of moral judgments that alienate people and divide communities.

Even one-night stands are not a violation of the third precept as long as you are not causing suffering for yourself or others. However, if you are using sex to satisfy a craving for pleasure, then you are trapped, because cravings, by their very nature, can never be satisfied.

Craving is a form of intoxication. When we feel that our life is out of control or we're experiencing some loss, we often look for immediate, intoxicating pleasure so we can lose ourselves. We alienate ourselves from others through overeating, overstimulation, incessant noise, and the need for constant entertainment. We are especially alienated, not only from others but even from ourselves, when it comes to sex.

Sex used as an intoxicant actually diminishes genuine pleasure and can trigger deep feelings of alienation, frustration, and even violence. Craving triggers alienation, and alienation triggers craving. This is a trap that many people fall into. Avoiding this trap is one key to staying on the path of a peaceful heart.

> KEY #3: Using sex as an intoxicant triggers feelings of alienation and diminishes genuine pleasure.

Any discussion of sexuality in the twenty-first century has to include lesbian, gay, bisexual, and transgender sexuality. Here again, Zen does not discriminate. It takes resilience and sensitivity to live in a world with people who have different beliefs, ideas, and sexual practices. Beliefs that are radically different from your own may seem peculiar or strange. I'm seventy-two years old. I was an adult when the gay rights movement began. As people began to open up publicly about their sexuality, the things I was learning about were so unfamiliar to me that they seemed unnatural. This was my opportunity to recognize that my heart and mind were split.

There's a story about a practitioner who said to his teacher, "I don't know what to do. I'm always getting into trouble when I'm around people. I don't want to condemn others, but I do it anyway. What can I do? I feel so out of balance."

The teacher replied, "When we live with others, we should not have sharp edges that hurt people. If you cannot stop condemning others, then you should not live in a community. But you should know that this is a weakness. When we are round, we can easily turn toward all. I live a solitary life, not because of my virtue but because of my weakness."

As this story implies, it takes a lot of inner strength and resilience to live in harmony with others. Living in community can feel like being in a rock tumbler. Our sharp edges are constantly being smoothed out through contact with those around us.

In many parts of the world, homophobia has a razor-sharp edge. Fear says, "The behavior that is familiar to me is natural; that other behavior is unnatural." But what is natural and unnatural? Interconnectedness is natural. Permeability is natural. It follows then that casting others out of our heart is not only unnatural but also increases our own feelings of isolation, confusion, and loneliness.

SEX AND INTIMACY

A man was deeply in love, but all his attempts to attract his lover failed. Secretly, he spent hours and hours writing long, heartrending letters to her, declaring his love and distress.

Finally, she agreed to go on a date. The man was delighted.

At long last, the man was sitting next to his beloved. He reached into his pocket for the letters he'd written and began to read them to her. They passionately expressed the pain he'd endured these past months and his longing to be with her.

As the hours passed he read on and on. Suddenly, his beloved interrupted him. She said, "What kind of fool are you? These letters are about me, about your longing for me! Here I'm sitting with you at last and you're lost in your stupid letters."

Austerity and indulgence are two coping strategies we use to avoid intimacy. How much of our chattering arises from fear of intimacy?

As I write this book, we are nearing a presidential election here in the United States. Everyone is talking about it. It's a safe topic because it's about our opinions, ideals, and ideas. We don't have to deal with our vulnerabilities or emotions. We are with others, but there's no intimacy. True intimacy has nothing to do with opinions, ideals, and ideas.

Paradoxically, sex can also be a barrier to intimacy. If we don't allow ourselves to be vulnerable during sex, there is no intimacy. Vulnerability is openness. It means we are open and receptive to our own pleasure *and* to our partner's pleasure. Being vulnerable actually doubles our sense of pleasure.

Even casual sex is more pleasurable and fulfilling if it involves intimacy, though the intimacy may be fleeting and somewhat superficial. Everything is fleeting anyway. In the next encounter, the opportunity for intimacy arises again.

Emotional health requires balance. A sexual relationship is neither appropriate nor healthy if it involves minors, people in mental institutions or prisons, or sex outside of a committed relationship. It may be ethically irresponsible in cases involving a power differential, such as a doctor/patient, employer/

employee, or teacher/student relationship. Other than that, from a Zen perspective, what you do with your body is your own affair, provided you are being compassionate toward yourself and others.

Is there a difference between promiscuity and casual or recreational sex? I think so. Promiscuity is associated with carelessness and indiscriminate, obsessive sexual behavior. Or, promiscuity may be a manifestation of neediness. When a person is promiscuous, there's often an underlying emotional issue that is being avoided. The close association between promiscuity and suffering should not be overlooked.

If we use sex to mask our insecurity or loneliness, then we feel cut off from everyone. If promiscuity is concealing an underlying fear of intimacy, then we are using sex to avoid commitment. Or maybe it's the opposite extreme: we are promiscuous because no one fits our vision of an ideal partner. Both extremes are fear-based, and both diminish the intrinsic joy of sex.

ORGASM, SATORI, AND MEDITATION

An orgasm is often compared to an ecstatic enlightenment experience, which in Zen is called *satori*. Both orgasm and satori share certain commonalities: time and thought stop, insecurities and concerns drop away, and the small self is forgotten. Both are altered states of consciousness, and both may be followed by a period of tranquility and crystalline awareness.

But there are also significant differences. Satori is an experience that arises from a deeply meditative state and may result in permanent life-altering change. Pleasure derived from meditative states and pleasure derived from orgasm light up different parts of the brain. Meditation lights up the left prefrontal cortex, which is associated with joy and happiness. During an orgasm, this area of the brain is dark. Research shows that a sustained meditation practice increases the amount of gray matter in our brain by thickening the prefrontal cortex, indicating a permanent change.

With meditation, pleasurable experiences arise from a sense of clarity, expansiveness, and spaciousness. We are aware of but not distracted by the arising and dissolving of thoughts, sensations, and feelings. Self-involvement tends to drop away as one senses the immediate presence of an immense reality. Often, colors are brighter and more intense. Objects may have a luminous, crystalline quality. Sounds may seem tangible. During satori, the body and mind are immersed in a sense of deep stillness and calm, whereas in an orgasm the bodily sensations are intense rather than calm; one's awareness is absorbed by the body rather than expanding beyond it.

Common to both ecstatic experiences is the dropping away of our mental involvement with a separate, isolated self. In 2011, *Scientific American* published an article titled "The Neurobiology of Bliss—Sacred and Profane," written by Nadia Webb. She wrote, "Bliss, both sacred and profane, shares the diminution of self-awareness, alterations in bodily perception, and decreased sense of pain." Webb described self-awareness as "a running critique," wherein storytelling is the cognitive default.

Luckily for Zen practitioners, we don't have to renounce either the profane or the sacred. With a balanced spiritual practice, we can enjoy both of these ecstatic pleasures that diminish our sense of a separate, isolated self.

SEX AND HUMOR IN RED THREAD ZEN

The Zen monk Ikkyu Sojun (1394–1481) was the illegitimate son of the emperor of Japan. He was raised in a Rinzai Zen monastery where the temple masters taught Chinese poetry, art, and literature.

As a young adult, Ikkyu left monastic life and became a mendicant monk, that is, a traveling beggar. He relentlessly attacked what he saw as politics and hypocrisy in the Zen establishment, especially the hypocritical attitude toward women and sexuality. According to Ikkyu, there was a lot of homosexual and heterosexual activity going on in the monasteries, but nobody talked about it. Some of the abbots had concubines who lived in small rooms in the back of the monastery.

For Ikkyu, the sacred was not separate from ordinary life. And ordinary life for Ikkyu included sake, meditation, and sex with both men and women. His students were monks, hobos, criminals, prostitutes, artists, and poets. He was given the nickname Crazy Cloud.

Crazy Cloud may be the most eccentric and iconoclastic monk in the history of Japanese Zen. He is considered one of the most famous flute players of medieval Japan. He also had a great influence on the Japanese tea ceremony and is renowned as one of medieval Japan's greatest calligraphers and literati (Chinese ink wash) painters. He practiced what he called Red Thread Zen, the Zen of passion.

Crazy Cloud's exuberance for the sacred, the profane, and for Zen without ceremony is expressed in his poetry:

Stilted koans and strained answers are all you have.
Forever pandering to officials and rich patrons.
Good friends of the Dharma, so proud,
But a brothel girl in gold brocade has you beat by a mile.

In Zen monasteries, then as now, they eat only vegetarian meals. Here is what Ikkyu had to say about that:

A MEAL OF FRESH OCTOPUS
Lots of arms, just like Kannon the Goddess;
Sacrificed for me, garnished with citron, I revere it so!
The taste of the sea, just divine!
Sorry, Buddha, this is another precept I just cannot keep.

Crazy Cloud also had a deep appreciation for the bodies of both
men and women, as the following two poems attest.

A MAN'S ROOT
Eight inches strong, it is my favorite thing;
If I'm alone at night, I embrace it fully—
A beautiful woman hasn't touched it for ages.
Within my *fundoshi** there is an entire universe!

A WOMAN'S SEX
It has the original mouth but remains wordless;
It is surrounded by a magnificent mound of hair.
Sentient beings can get completely lost in it
But it is also the birthplace of all the Buddhas of the
ten thousand worlds.

Long ago, there was an old woman who had been supporting
a hermit monk for twenty years. She had a sixteen-year-old girl
bring him meals. One day, she instructed the girl to embrace
the monk and ask, "How do you feel right now?" The young girl
did as she was told, and the monk's response was, "I'm an old
withered tree against a frigid cliff on the coldest day of winter."
When the girl returned and repeated the monk's words, the
old woman exclaimed, "For twenty years I've been supporting

* Wrapped thong-style men's underwear.

that base worldling!" The old woman chased the monk out and set the hermitage on fire.

Ikkyu wrote a poem in response to this story.

> The old woman was bighearted enough
> To elevate the pure monk with a girl to wed.
> Tonight if a beauty were to embrace me
> My withered old willow branch would sprout a new shoot!

As Ikkyu aged, he began to settle down. He quit going to whorehouses and eventually fell in love with a blind singer named Mori, who was quite a bit younger than he. They were together for the rest of Ikkyu's life. He wrote poetry about this, too.

> Every night, Blind Mori accompanies me in song.
> Under the covers, two mandarin ducks whisper to each
> other.
> We promise to be together forever,
> But right now this old fellow enjoys an eternal spring.

LADY MORI'S GIFTED TOUCH
> My hand is no match for that of Mori.
> She is the unrivaled master of love play:
> When my jade stalk wilts, she can make it sprout!
> How we enjoy our intimate little circle.

TO LADY MORI WITH DEEPEST GRATITUDE AND THANKS
> The tree was barren of leaves but you brought a new spring.
> Long green sprouts, verdant flowers, fresh promise.
> Mori, if I ever forget my profound gratitude to you,
> Let me burn in hell forever.

The Zen emphasis is on being naturally human. We make mistakes. We screw things up. We get angry, become anxious, and do stupid things. As Zen practitioners, we bring our fear to the meditation cushion and find some freedom for a few minutes. But then it comes back and follows us around.

This is the human situation. We can't escape it. But when we show up for it, with nonjudgmental awareness, we can experience the wonderfully chaotic ocean of life surrounding, penetrating, and supporting us even when we feel overwhelmed by it.

SEX IN THE AMERICAN ZEN COMMUNITY

So far, I have been speaking about Zen values in a general sense. And generally speaking, Zen in America is doing pretty well, concerning issues around gender and sexuality. But at the teacher level, we have had some major failures.

A sexual relationship between a teacher and a student is a betrayal of Buddha's teachings. This is not a moralistic view; it is a practical one. A teacher/student relationship is based on a commitment to honor the teachings of Buddha.

There is a well-known story about a woman who told Suzuki Roshi that she had feelings of deep love for him. Suzuki replied, "It is okay to feel whatever you feel for your teacher. I have enough discipline for both of us." That is the role of the teacher. Suzuki didn't judge, lecture, or make the woman feel awkward or weird about her emotions. Emotions are just emotions. We can't repress or suppress them. But we can learn to deal with them skillfully and with some maturity and compassion.

In Zen, we learn to honor both the individual and the undivided nature of all life. If we don't appreciate a thing's individual nature, which we can see and experience in an immediate and personal way, then how can we appreciate its undivided nature, which is beyond ordinary experience? When we appreciate every person and object we encounter, then each moment has the potential to deepen our capacity for intimacy.

Once, a samurai, after committing himself to Zen, asked his teacher, "How long can I carry my sword?"

The Zen master replied, "As long as you can."

When ordinary life is not separate from the sacred, everything becomes our teacher. The Zen master knew that when the sword has taught and the samurai has learned, he will look down one day and notice that it is no longer at his side.

DOING THE WORK

If you are struggling to find balance around issues involving sex and intimacy, please consider the following questions. They will help you to embody the core Buddhist teachings and to cultivate clarity, balance, and poise within your unique situation.

1. Have you used sex to mask your insecurity or loneliness?
2. Are you using sex to avoid commitment?
3. Do you find yourself in a series of sexual relationships not for the intrinsic pleasure of being with the person but because you're searching for the ideal partner?

To cultivate a more harmonious life and/or discover your own razor-sharp edges, consider the following exercises and questions.

1. For the next week, pay attention to your tendency to bounce between deprivation and self-indulgence, whether it's with food, sex, or anything else. Don't judge yourself. As you notice, breathe and open yourself up to any anxiety, fear, or other emotion, especially one that triggers the opposite extreme.

2. Notice any rules of behavior that you have internalized or tried to internalize, such as, I will only have chocolate once a week, or, I will not yell at my best friend when I am angry. How does that rule support you in your attempt to be open and receptive? How does the rule impede your openness? Be specific.

3. Look closely at your attitude toward different approaches to sexuality or types of sexual expression. Has it stayed the same or changed over time? Within your oceanic consciousness, can you find room to accept any and all types of sexuality, as long as they don't involve suffering?

FOUR

Money

Having enough money to ensure one's basic needs is vital for happiness. However, many of us are convinced that more money means more happiness. The "more is better" seed is sown far and wide in the United States, and it gets plenty of sun and water. Often it is rooted in a deeply ingrained sense of scarcity, a belief that there's only so much prosperity to go around: the more you get, the less there is for me.

We may not buy into the more-is-better assumption on a conscious level, but it's a core value in our culture, and its influence is everywhere. The message is spread on freeway billboards across America, on TV, in song lyrics, in magazines. Celebrities show off their elaborate homes, and the term *mega-mansion* is now a part of our vocabulary.

Research shows an interesting correlation between money and happiness: Adding money to money does not buy more happiness. In fact, having too much money may actually lessen our experience of happiness. "This may be because when we think

we're well off, a sense of complacency settles in, making everything seem a bit dull," said Amit Kumar, a researcher at Cornell
University.*

I think having too much of anything lessens our capacity for
happiness. The most powerful contributor to personal happiness
is the quality of our relationships. In Zen, abundance is about
relationship, not ownership.

MONEYLESS SOCIETIES

In chapter two, I introduced the concept of infinite worthiness
as a core Buddhist value. Historically, in the United States and
throughout the world, small pockets of moneyless societies have
aspired to reflect that fundamental virtue. Unfortunately, most
of them have failed.

One such effort began in the fifth century with state-run monasteries in China. To actualize the teaching that all life is interdependent, everyone in the monastery was considered of equal worth
and treated accordingly. Therefore, everything was shared equally.
Hierarchy existed, but it was secondary to the ideal of interdependence, equality, and the ethos of generosity. Unfortunately, these
Chinese monasteries are no longer in existence. Archeological evidence suggests they fizzled out by the seventh century.

More recent efforts to create moneyless societies have sprung
up around the world in the form of state-run systems and small
collectives. In Israel, the kibbutz movement began in 1948. The
word means "communal settlement," and many kibbutzim still
exist today. Scandinavian communes have also been somewhat
successful.

* David DiSalvo, "The Latest Science on Whether Money Can Buy Happiness,"
Forbes, February 28, 2015, https://www.forbes.com/sites/daviddisalvo/2015/02/28
/does-anyone-really-know-if-money-can-buy-happiness/#7a62b78d7d71.

In the United States, communal living was a popular aspect of the sixties counterculture. After my wife, Linda, and I moved to Minnesota in 1969, our family of four lived communally with another family for three years. Then our experiment in communal living fizzled out, as did most of the others.

Why does communal living so frequently fail? Maybe poet T. S. Eliot had it right when he wrote, "Between the idea and the reality falls the shadow."

As human beings, we are hardwired, culturally and genetically, to take care of ourselves and our families. A spiritual practice that ignores this hardwiring is doomed because real life happens on the ground and in the body, not in our ideals.

Many communal societies fizzled out because they were based on a single idea: share the wealth. They didn't take into account our natural impulse to put the well-being of ourselves and our loved ones first. This deeply ingrained imperative was ignored or repressed, but it didn't dissolve. A natural consequence was passive-aggressiveness, hidden agendas, shame, guilt, and even violence.

I apprenticed for a while with a Lakota medicine man named Elmer Running. *Mitákuye Oyás'in* is a Lakota expression that means "all my relatives." It refers to our inherent connectedness and the infinite worth of all things. A grain of sand, a tree, the statesman, and an indigent person all have equal value. This principle is actualized in the daily lives of the Lakota through generosity; the underlying dictate is "to give."

Once when I met with Elmer he reeked of alcohol. But Elmer didn't drink. "You smell like a brewery," I said. "What's going on?"

Elmer explained. Earlier that day a group of guys had gathered at a friend's house. This friend had recently been gifted a case of beer, and he didn't want to give it away. So he hid it in the oven. When his wife came home unexpectedly, she turned on the gas and lit the oven. Shortly thereafter: Ka-boom! Beer splatter went everywhere, including all over Elmer. His friend's clever plan to avoid being generous with his beer had backfired.

Our basic ego needs can't be suppressed for long. The more we cling to ideals that ignore or deny our instinctual drives, the darker the shadow. T. S. Eliot warns us that we can't ignore the shadow side of being human. Our most altruistic idealists are often thrown off balance by it.

MARXISM, CAPITALISM, AND ZEN

From each according to his ability, to each according to his needs.

—KARL MARX

During the last century, two predominant economies have battled for global supremacy: Marxism and capitalism. Capitalism has clearly won out, but there's still a little Marxism here and there. Being a Marxist in the United States used to be okay, but disdain for totalitarian communism like that practiced in the former USSR and in China has soured American attitudes toward Marxism.

The slogan penned by nineteenth-century economist Karl Marx sounds like a poetic expression of Zen values. However, Marxism does not include the principle of infinite worth or the interdependence of all life. In Zen, we don't differentiate between the spiritual and material, or between the end and the means. If all things are infinitely worthy just as they are, there's no need to get all wigged out about the equal production and distribution of material goods. If we are truly actualizing the principle of infinite worth, we take care of each other naturally, without creating artificial boundaries between the physical and the spiritual, or between the collective and the individual: what is good for the individual is good for the collective. From a Zen perspective, the Marxist focus on material equality appears misguided.

In the seventies, people didn't know whether the seeds of Zen would sprout in American soil. Looking at Zen's history, one might feel a bit dubious about its future. Zen is no longer flourishing in its motherland, China, or in its secondary homeland, Japan. Where, then, is it flourishing?

Zen is flourishing right here in the most ardent capitalist country in the world. This makes sense. In contrast to many Buddhist countries, the United States was founded by people from different cultures with diverse ideas about how we should live. By necessity, our founders created a set of principles that encourage us to let go of our fixations and learn to live together. A common metaphor for America is a melting pot. But I think a better metaphor is the mosaic. In a mosaic, different colors and textures are not fused into one colorless whole. Instead, each piece is appreciated as it is, complemented rather than diminished by those around it. A mosaic creates a delicate and complex balance wherein each individual tile is both independent and interdependent.

In American culture, our democratic roots place great value on individual effort. Likewise, Zen practice requires great individual effort to still the mind and open the heart, which returns us naturally to our original interdependence. While rugged individualism is a core value in American culture, there is also the recognition that our strength lies not only in our independence but also in our interdependence. Traditions like the community barn-raising or the New England town meeting speak to this side of our culture. Zen practice can help us honor this interplay between independence and interdependence in a way that supports and strengthens the American way of life.

Twenty-first-century America is a big-time money economy. Our attitudes and our economy have become global. In modern capitalist societies like the United States, there are three different ways in which people can labor. We can think of these as alternative rails. The first rail is the for-profit sector. The second is the public sector. The third is the nonprofit sector.

The nonprofit sector, the third rail, is flourishing more in America than in any other country in the world—and more than in all the European countries combined. Theoretically, nonprofits are driven not by dollars but by mission. A focus on mission allows interdependence to be actualized through reciprocity, whether you work for a nonprofit or you contribute to one.

Notice I said "theoretically." I'm not ignoring what actually happens on the ground. Nonprofits are run by human beings, after all, so even here we cannot ignore the shadow. Desire for material enrichment sometimes lurks beneath the surface of a nonprofit organization. Still, the underlying ideal of helping others sustains the nonprofit sector. It's not so hard to manifest the principle of infinite worth when helping others is the mission.

The first rail, the for-profit sector, is also based on reciprocity. A business or corporation sells a product or provides a service that others can use and benefit from. But the underlying imperative here is financial gain. Americans who practice Zen and work in the for-profit sector may experience tension between the primary profit motive of corporate life and the core value of infinite worth.

On the other hand, there are businesses in the for-profit sector that focus primarily on delivering high-quality products or services, trusting that profit will follow. The attitude is that financial success will be a by-product of the devotion to a quality-driven mission.

At my high school in Palo Alto, I was on the cross-country running team with a guy named Walter Hewlett. His dad, Bill Hewlett, was an engineer who was fascinated with the possibility of creating technology to help people communicate more efficiently, more clearly, and more respectfully. He hired people who had a similar vision. He treated them well and paid them well, even though he had little money and they were working in his garage.

Bill Hewlett had a deep respect for the potential of technology. He and his partner Dave Packard worked collaboratively with the small group of engineers in Bill's garage to develop a vision and direction for the company. That was the beginning of Hewlett-Packard. Many people consider it the beginning of what we know as Silicon Valley.

Bill Hewlett died in 2001. In the ensuing years, Hewlett-Packard went through a difficult time. Arguably, the difficulty arose because the company lost its mission-driven imperative to connect people through technology.

A few years later, I got a little insight into Hewlett's character. I was back in the Bay Area visiting my elderly dad, who was ill and had become frail. He could no longer take care of himself, so he had a caretaker.

My dad grew cantankerous as he aged. The older he got, the crankier he became. It hurt me to watch how badly he treated people. Once, after he'd berated his caretaker, I tried to console her.

"I wish Bill Hewlett hadn't died," she said sadly.

"You knew Bill Hewlett?" I asked.

"Yes, before I worked for your dad I worked for Mr. Hewlett. He was so wonderful. Even though he couldn't walk, he cared only about my well-being when I came to work. He always asked if I'd had my lunch. He couldn't even get out of bed to fix my lunch, but he always had ideas about how I could get my lunch." She paused for a moment, as if lost in a memory about her old boss.

Then she added, "Now I'm stuck with your dad."

According to Suzuki Roshi, the labor itself is important, not the accumulation of wealth. "Labor makes sense," Suzuki said, "when you work on things with respect. That should be the true nature of labor." However, Suzuki added, "to value your labor over the materials you are given is arrogant." Balancing these underlying attitudes about money, labor, and materialism is how we're able to remain fluid, generous, and engaged in a capitalistic society. It is also how we manifest the interdependent nature and infinite worthiness of the people and things in our everyday life.

I remember a conversation I had many years ago with Katagiri Roshi, founder of the Minnesota Zen Meditation Center (MZMC). We were in a meeting, waiting for a couple of people who hadn't arrived yet.

"They're late because they were going to a TGIF party," I said.

"What's that?" Katagiri asked.

"Thank God it's Friday," I explained.

Katagiri was confused. The concept of separating our work week from the rest of our life didn't make sense to him. I tried to explain it several times, but it was so foreign to the Zen attitude and Katagiri's way of being in the world that he couldn't get it. Whatever labor we do gives us life and gives life to others. There is intrinsic pleasure and intrinsic worth if we just give ourselves to each activity. So he never understood why Americans should feel the need for a TGIF party.

MONEY IN BUDDHIST THOUGHT

Once Buddha was asked by a landowner, "What should I do with my land?" Buddha replied, "Don't let your property sit idle. Plant crops on your land."

Buddha wanted us to use what we have to add vitality to the world. When we are generous, we feel wealthy. No matter how wealthy a person is on the outside, if they are not generous they won't *feel* their wealth. A hoarder doesn't feel wealthy. He experiences scarcity. He may think he is wealthy in his mind, but he doesn't feel it in his heart, and so he is driven to hoard more and more things. But what good is it to own a lot of things if you always have the feeling of *not enough*?

A grain of sand and the entire beach, a refugee tent and the Taj Mahal: each is a manifestation of an interdependent, interchangeable network of life. Our interest is in supporting the dynamic vitality of this ongoing interchange. Yet we live in a culture where money sets specific values. How do we reconcile these opposing paradigms within our own hearts and minds?

Here again, we can use some guidance from Suzuki Roshi:

Life is always about exchange. A genuine exchange is a
    purification in which
the person who gives doesn't feel that he doesn't owe
    anything anymore.

—SUZUKI ROSHI

I would add that the person who receives doesn't feel that he doesn't deserve anything anymore. So it's an open process, a matter of continuous engagement in an exchange system based on mutual respectfulness. Bill Hewlett continually gave without a lot of thought about where he was going or what he would get back. But he got back a lot. After achieving financial success, he established the William and Flora Hewlett Foundation as a means of continuously giving back. At its best, our capitalist system can be an open process of continuous giving and receiving.

According to Suzuki, life is a continuous flow of give and take, and money is a symbolic form of this exchange. It follows, then, that money should be understood as a by-product of this interchange, rather than a possession within itself. As such, money does not really belong to anyone.

Our fourth Key for living an abundant life comes from the teachings of Suzuki Roshi.

> KEY #4: Money is not yours—
> it belongs to society.

When we labor with respect for the work being done, value is added. When we conduct our exchanges with respect for the labor of others, value is added. Not the kind of value that increases the bottom line but a much richer and deeper value, an abundance that you feel in your heart rather than hold in your bank account. The value you add through respect for the labor of others affirms life and is the primary source of true abundance.

I'll end this chapter by describing seven qualities Buddha recommended to cultivate the kind of abundance the heart recognizes. Those qualities are conviction, virtue, conscience, breadth of learning, generosity, discernment, and scrupulousness.

Conviction. When I started out, I wasn't a very good Zen student. I was clumsy. I was absentminded. I made mistakes. But I had conviction and I was determined. Suzuki said to me once, "Because of your determination you will be able to see and become the reality that includes all life."

Determination comes from conviction, and conviction starts with a belief. I believed the words of my teacher. I watered and nurtured that belief by showing up for meditation and for dharma talks, and by hanging out with others who felt the same way.

Virtue. From a Zen perspective, virtue is about not separating the means from the end. It is the realization that, at each point along the way, the path and the destination are the same. From a Zen point of view, how you get there is where you are going. When we separate the means from the end, our heart splinters—and no amount of money can heal a splintered heart.

Conscience. Early in life, our moral compass may come from our parents or our culture, but eventually we have to develop our own compass, one that arises from a subtle and nuanced regard for the world. In good conscience, we can't fail to notice and appreciate the beauty of a flower or the setting sun or a smile, and so there is a sense of boundless camaraderie, not just with other sentient beings but with all that exists. From this perspective, a fully developed sense of conscience becomes a wellspring of abundance.

Inner wealth is about feeling our connectedness. It fills us up so there is no sense of scarcity or of lacking anything at all. When we are filled up, outer wealth can't compare to the joyfulness that may suddenly arise from simply noticing the color of the sky, the shape of a cloud, or the patterns formed by falling leaves. A fully developed conscience allows us to sink into our lives and experience the freshness that is always there.

Breadth of learning. We can't neglect the intellect in our practice. Intellectual learning allows us to help people.

There's a familiar story about four blind men who approach an elephant. The one who approaches from the front feels the elephant's trunk and thinks it is a hose; the man on the side thinks he is touching a wall; the one behind the elephant examines the tail and concludes it is a broom; and the fourth mistakes an ear for a fan. Then the four friends get into a brawl over who is right.

Breadth of learning allows us to see things from multiple perspectives. If we understand how a person could mistake an elephant for a broom or a wall, then we're in a position to help them move beyond their confusion.

My daughter, Erin, spent years learning about other cultures. She wanted to understand how people of different cultures could work together more effectively. Now her book *The Culture Map* is helping thousands of people across the globe appreciate the values and customs of others.

Generosity. As I suggested earlier, when we give things ungrudgingly and wholeheartedly, we feel wealthy. We tap into our connectedness to the person or cause we give to, and beyond this to all humanity and quite possibly all life.

Wholehearted giving is different from conditioned giving. When you give out of habit or because you think you're supposed to, then you are clinging to some idea. It's okay to give because you feel you're supposed to—but inner wealth is cultivated only when we give wholeheartedly. "In the godhead there is no thought of God," said the German mystic Meister Eckhart. When your hand is all the way open, there is no thought of generosity.

Discernment. When striving for outer wealth, discernment involves measuring, judging, analyzing, and comparing. But in meditation, discernment has a very different quality. We attempt to carefully notice each thought, sensation, and emotion as it arises, without measuring, judging, analyzing, and comparing. Meditative discernment requires a very subtle and composed mind. If you bring to the cushion the same discerning mind you use in the outer world, inner discernment is lost.

Scrupulousness. The saying "God is in the details" suggests that we should be meticulous in all our affairs. But scrupulousness goes beyond being meticulous. A good bank robber is meticulous, but he is not scrupulous. Scrupulousness is a quality that combines a fully developed sense of conscience with what Buddha referred to as *upaya*, which translates as "skillfulness" or "skillful means." Scrupulousness involves the integration of the other six qualities.

The following journaling practice, developed by Dr. Rachel Naomi Remen, a teacher of alternative medicine, can help you discover the infinite worthiness that is already present in your life. If you do this practice with sincerity, I think the results will surprise you.

Take ten minutes before going to bed to reflect on your day. Looking backward, review your day by writing in a journal. For instance, "I watched the evening news on TV. I checked my e-mails. I had dinner. I drove home from work. I had lunch with a colleague. I had a meeting with my boss. I drove to work. I had breakfast. I took a shower. I woke up." You'll want to be a little more detailed than this, but you get the point.

You'll be asking three questions as you reflect on this list of activities. First: What surprised me today? Go back through the list and find something and write it down.

Then start the review again with the question: What touched my heart today? Write it down.

Finally, review your day again with the third question: What inspired me today? Write it out.

If you have difficulty with these questions, consider that the problem is not in your activities but in the way you're thinking about your activities. Dr. Remen advises that you think like a storyteller or a poet. Look deeply into the events of your day. Who made you smile, and why? When you kissed your spouse, partner, or children this morning, was it from the heart? Were you touched by it?

A couple of weeks into this practice, you may notice that you only seem to find meaning and value in your life several hours later, when you sit down with your journal. But eventually, that gap will close. That is the power of this exercise.

FIVE

Failure Is Just
an Experience

*Failure stripped away everything inessential. It taught me
things about myself I could have learned no other way.*

—J. K. ROWLING

J. K. ROWLING, THE NOVELIST who created the
Harry Potter book series, recognizes the power of
failure. Failure can help us to develop certain qualities necessary for personal, professional, and spiritual growth—qualities
like coping skills, emotional resilience, creative thinking, and
the ability to collaborate. While success encourages us to keep
doing the same thing, to stick to our routine or formula, failure
forces us to open up to new ideas, to reach out to others, and to
go beyond our comfort zone.

Unfortunately, our culture takes a dim view of failure.
Americans live in a very competitive culture—so much so that
life often feels like a contest filled with big winners and big
losers. In business, sports, and the arts, we tend to worship
winners and marginalize those who fail. So how do we cope

with failure? Perhaps we need a cultural shift in the way we think about failure.

When I was a kid, I had to do an hour of work a week. In the summer, my job was pulling dandelions from the lawn, and it seemed to me that every week there were twice as many dandelions as the week before.

Surprisingly, dandelions fail to germinate five times more often than they succeed. That is an extraordinary failure rate. However, based on diversity and perseverance, they also have an extraordinary success rate. Botanists have identified about a hundred different types of dandelion. You'll find them sprouting up from fallow dirt or rich soil, and they thrive at both sea level and high altitudes. Consequently, the humble dandelion has been around for thirty million years.

So that's the deal with dandelions. What about human beings?

Ernest Hemingway wrote the ending to his novel *A Farewell to Arms* forty-seven times. That means forty-six consecutive failures—but he persevered. Thomas Edison failed with a thousand different filaments before he found the one that enabled him to create the first successful incandescent lightbulb.

We humans have an extraordinary failure rate—but we also have an extraordinary success rate.

When Michael Jordan tried out for his high school basketball team, he didn't make it. Then he started practicing every day. When he tried out in college, he still didn't make the A team, but he kept practicing. Michael Jordan finally became *Michael Jordan*—after he failed, adapted, and persevered.

> Whenever I was working out and got tired and figured I ought to stop, I'd close my eyes and see that list in the locker room without my name on it. That usually got me going again.
>
> —MICHAEL JORDAN

So maybe failure is a prerequisite for success. Maybe dandelions survived *because* of their extraordinary failure rate rather than in spite of it. They were forced to adapt, to venture into new territory, and to diversify. Likewise, perhaps the most successful people are those who fail the most. You could say that persistence in failure is what success is all about.

The research of Jonathan Hay, a psychologist at the University of Virginia, suggests that happiness may require adversity, setbacks, and even trauma. "If you don't get the kind of information failure provides," Hay says, "you will end up with unrealistic expectations."

FAILING WITHOUT ATTACHMENT TO FAILURE

Nevertheless, it's not easy to simply roll with our mistakes, to fail without becoming emotionally attached to our failures. Instead of learning and adapting, we often get caught up in guilt or shame. Guilt is okay; it means failure was due to something we did. We take responsibility and feel guilty about not doing as well as we should have. As long as we don't cling to the guilt feelings, they can motivate us to try a different approach.

But shame is not cool. When we feel shame, we attribute failing to something we *are* rather something we did. We take on a negative label. Be careful of the kind of self-talk that criticizes and condemns. Don't believe it. If you do, you won't try anything new—you'll just freeze up and fall back on some routine that dulls you out.

A few years ago, a man started coming to our Zen center just after his marriage fell apart. This is a common practice; a lot of people want to learn meditation because they are failing in marriage. As he worked through the challenges of his marriage within the framework of a meditation practice, he began to see how he could do things differently next time. Now he is in another marriage. So far, so good.

"People sometimes seize such opportunities," Hay says, "rebuilding beautifully those parts of their lives and life stories that they could never have torn down voluntarily." So it's important for us to believe we can learn from failure, and seize our opportunities to rebuild.

We used to think that IQ, which supposedly measures intelligence, was a fixed quantity that remained constant your whole life. But research shows that intelligence is malleable. Carol Dweck, author of *Mindset: The New Psychology of Success*, is a Stanford psychologist who works with kids and their parents. She teaches parents to value their child's failures because failing is how we learn.

Dweck instructs parents and teachers not to label kids. Even positive labels, such as "smart," can be limiting. Instead, Dweck encourages parents and teachers to praise kids for their effort.

In a study described in the *Journal of Personality and Social Psychology*, Dweck asked four hundred fifth-graders to complete a set of puzzles. Along the way, one group was praised for being smart. The other group was praised for their effort. After a few easy puzzles, the students were given a difficult one, which neither group was able to complete. Afterward, they were given easy ones again. The "smart" group was so discouraged by their previous failure that they did 20 percent worse than they had on the initial round. The group praised for their effort did 30 percent better.

If we become attached to praise, we're conditioning ourselves to depend on others for validation. Attachment to praise means we require a constant flow of praise to feel worthy and valued.

> You get confidence from overcoming adversity, not from being told how great you are all the time.
>
> —DAN KINDLON, PHD

Buddha talked about the eight worldly winds: praise and blame, success and failure, pleasure and pain, fame and disrepute. Buddhist psychology says that experiencing equally the eight worldly winds without fixating on any one of them cultivates a sense of well-being, emotional maturity, and spiritual freedom.

Fixation, however, does seem to be a deeply ingrained habit of the human psyche. Research has shown that even smells can become associated with failure and condition people to fail.

At the Monell Chemical Senses Center in Philadelphia, researchers asked two groups of volunteers to enter an impossible maze. The researchers wanted to guarantee the experience of failing.

One group was exposed to a subtle floral scent as they tried and failed to navigate the maze. The control group was not exposed to the scent. Next time, both groups entered a simple maze infused with the floral scent. The control group found their way out of the maze easily. But those who had come to associate the floral scent with failure were unable to navigate it.

With a regular meditation practice, we begin to see how quickly we fixate and project into the future specific aspects of our past experience. A daily meditation practice exposes us repeatedly to our attachments. Over and over, our mind attaches to some idea or concept. Over and over, we let go and return. In the beginning, and often for a long time, we judge, compare, feel frustrated, and condemn ourselves. Eventually, we begin to see the passing nature of things. The real work of meditation is just seeing, without attaching or rejecting. But for many of us, clinging to this and rejecting that has become a way of life.

LEARNING TO FAIL SKILLFULLY

They are forever free who renounce all selfish desires
and break away from the ego cage of "I," "me," and "mine."

—BHAGAVAD GITA

Americans have been treated like consumers for a long time. Self-indulgence has become a conditioned cultural value. Our status and possessions are measures of our worthiness. These values benefit corporate America, but what about us? Paradoxically, the key to lasting fulfillment is renunciation. Renunciation is a matter of putting aside our immediate desires just a little bit in order to focus on something bigger.

In a well-known experiment led by psychologist Walter Mischel, a group of four-year-olds were given one marshmallow. They were told by an adult that they could eat the marshmallow now if they wanted but if they waited until the adult returned, they would get two marshmallows. Then they were left alone with the marshmallow for fifteen minutes. Most could not resist; but about one out of three waited. The kids who waited did all sorts of things to distract themselves: some sang songs, others tried to nap, some even licked the marshmallow—but they didn't eat it.

The preschoolers from this study were tracked into adulthood. The results: The children who were able to wait for the greater reward became more adept at coping with frustration and stress. For those who couldn't wait, failure became a constant companion.

Fortunately, it's never too late to discover what the pain of failure is trying to teach us.

> KEY #5: Learning to fail skillfully
> involves renunciation.

Training in renunciation allows us to see our desires as they arise without indulging them. If you indulge a desire, what happens next? Another desire arises. And another and another. The faster you indulge your desires, the faster they come. What happens to your life in all this chasing around?

There is an alternative. If you investigate desire rather than indulge it, the pattern is broken. As your awareness expands, the stream of desire slows to a trickle. It never dries up completely, but it loses its power.

If a person gives way to all their desires, or panders to them, there will be no inner struggle in them, no friction, and no fire. But if for the sake of attaining liberation they struggle with their habits that hinder them they'll create a fire, which will gradually transform their inner world into a single whole.

—G. I. GURDJIEFF

Pandering to our desires distracts us from the inner struggle that failure often brings. In failure, we feel lost; we don't know which way to go. Living skillfully involves learning how to experience this discomfort.

After the publication of my first book, *Nothing Holy about It*, I spent a month in the San Francisco Bay Area promoting it. While I was there, I went hiking whenever I could. Once, I got lost in the Santa Cruz Mountains. I had my iPhone with me, but I was in a dead zone where no cell service was available. For several hours, I was lost. Eventually, little animal trails led me to bigger trails and finally back to a main road.

I had hiked the Santa Cruz Mountains throughout my childhood, but when I was lost, I felt as if I was seeing them for the first time. They were beautiful in ways I'd never noticed before.

Is it possible to enjoy not knowing which way to go? To walk slowly instead of running headlong toward a goal? When we embrace being lost, we may discover little paths that lead to new possibilities. In today's world, we don't have time to explore—but being lost forces us to take time. I found it joyful to follow the animal trails. We never know for sure which way to go, but that's life.

You lose yourself, you reappear
You suddenly find you got nothing to fear

—BOB DYLAN

So how can we be skillful and lost at the same time?

When my son, Jed, was born, he was not happy to be in this world. He was jaundiced and had to stay in the hospital for a total blood transfusion. When he came home, he was only happy when he was being nursed. He cried continuously except when he was nursing.

His mother and I were lost. We fumbled around, trying lots of things. We tried swaddling him, giving him warm baths, taking him on hikes. The hikes helped, but every time we stopped to rest, he cried. We were exhausted—plus we got lost. We didn't know which way to turn.

After weeks of being lost and fumbling around, we discovered the vacuum cleaner. When it was on, he stopped crying. Leaving the vacuum cleaner on—that's the secret we discovered. What a relief!

Being lost means you're out of your comfort zone. It means you've gone beyond the contours of your conditioned, fear-based thinking. The most formidable thresholds often feel like chasms, impossible to cross.

In September 2015, tennis player Roberta Vinci faced Serena Williams at the US Open. The odds against her were three hundred to one. On the court, she tried not to think about the scope of the challenge. Instead, she thought, "Hit the ball and run. Don't think, and run."

The next day, the headlines read, "Roberta Vinci Ends Serena Williams's Grand Slam Bid at US Open."

In an interview after the match, Vinci was asked, "When you woke up this morning, what gave you the belief that this moment was possible?"

Vinci explained that she *hadn't* believed it was possible. "In my mind I say, put the ball on the court. Don't think and try to put all the ball on the court."

Focused effort, renunciation, and trust are three hallmarks of skillful living. They help keep your brain from getting in your way. Just hit the ball and run. In his book *The Inner Game of Tennis*, W. Timothy Gallwey wrote,

> When one is emotionally attached to results that he cannot control, he tends to become anxious, and then tries too hard. But one can control the effort he puts into winning. One can always do the best he can at any given moment. Since it is impossible to feel anxiety about an event that one can control, the mere awareness that you are using maximum effort to win each point will carry you past the problem of anxiety.

WHEN YOU FAIL, FALL ALL THE WAY TO THE GROUND

Meeting failure informs your life below the conscious level. That means failure cannot be turned into a technique. If you think of failure as a technique, you are not truly meeting it. You're trying to mold it, rather than allowing your experience to mold you.

The willingness to fall all the way to the ground requires trust that the loss gives you as much power as the win. Falling all the way to the ground means accepting your failure completely. It is the willingness to look directly at the actions and motivations that got you here. Learning to see clearly requires meeting failure at every turn, without avoiding its emotional impact through denial, blaming others, or running toward a new goal.

When we accept failure completely, without qualification, it strips us of all the inessentials. We have the opportunity to return to our deepest level of being. Then, when we meditate, we become focused without even trying. We're not all over the place thinking about what we're going to do. We sink all the way into the ground and we stay there until we are renewed.

Forget your perfect offering
There is a crack, a crack in everything
That's how the light gets in.

—LEONARD COHEN, "ANTHEM"

THE NEW SCIENCE OF POST-TRAUMATIC GROWTH

The world breaks everyone and afterward many are strong at the broken places.

—ERNEST HEMINGWAY

The term *post-traumatic stress disorder* came into use in the 1970s and was officially recognized by the American Psychiatric Association (APA) in 1980. It affects 7 to 8 percent of Americans.

Until recently, the APA focused primarily on identifying diseases and maladies. But that has begun to change due to the influence of people like the Dalai Lama. He challenged scientists to devote their time to studying qualities that create well-being. It makes sense, doesn't it?

Today a new way of thinking is emerging, and along with it a new science: the science of post-traumatic growth (PTG). The term was coined in 1995 by psychologists Richard Tedeschi and Lawrence Calhoun from the University of North Carolina, but the phenomenon has been recognized for centuries. Finally scientists are looking seriously at why some people not only bounce back from tragedy but actually bounce *higher* than they were before.

It turns out we are hardwired to grow in the wake of tragedies and traumas—not from the events themselves but from the personal struggle that comes afterward. According to Tedeschi, the most fragile among us are often more open to positive changes following a tragedy. "If someone is already resilient, he doesn't need to change so drastically. PTG involves big change."

Tedeschi and Calhoun identified five forms of growth involved in PTG:

- People become more open to new opportunities
- They have an increased sense of inner strength
- Their relationships deepen
- Their appreciation for life increases
- They often report a renewed interest in spiritual life

Some people grow in all of these areas, others one or more.

PTG is a natural phenomenon, not a technique or an avoidance strategy. It is not about avoiding the painful feelings of loss, anger, and grief. The grieving process is difficult but necessary, and a supportive environment is important. You need a mentor, teacher, or a wise friend who can help you be kind to yourself, who can help you cross the threshold of your painful emotions again and again until you're flowing with them. Bringing kind awareness to your broken places evokes authentic compassion. You begin to trust yourself, and trust reignites your aspiration. Instead of wallowing in your pain, you slowly move back into the flow of life.

When you experience a big failure, it often feels that everything stops, that there is no movement to flow into. But the current is there. Maybe it's an undercurrent, pulling you deeper than you want to go.

If the undercurrent is strong, you can do turtle practice. When a turtle rests, it draws its legs, tail, and head inside its shell so there is no contact with the outer world. In turtle practice, we draw in our senses of sight, sound, taste, smell, and touch. As thoughts arise, just let them pass, over and over, until you enter into a state of quiet. Take time every day to do your turtle meditation until you begin to see things with radiance and clarity.

FROM FAILURE TO CLEAR-SEEING: I CAN SEE FOR MILES AND MILES

The Catholic mystic Henri Nouwen once said, "The friend who can be silent with us in a moment of despair or confusion, who can stay with us in an hour of grief or bereavement, who can tolerate not knowing, not curing, not healing, and face with us the reality of our powerlessness, that is a friend who cares." Ironically, the friend who can tolerate not knowing is also the friend who knows. She understands and accepts the chaos and uncertainty of life.

We all need a wise friend who can help us face a reality that includes failure and suffering. Setbacks, tragedies, and traumas are not to be denied or escaped. They are innate aspects of being human. When met with courage and compassion, they are paths to awakening.

When we stay with our meditation practice regardless of what is happening—praise or blame, success or failure, pleasure or despair—three shifts happen naturally.

The first is the shift from, What do I want to get from my meditation practice? to, What can I learn about myself in this practice? This shift is actually facilitated by failure. It is where we begin to see the fear-based thinking, judgments, and beliefs that drive our destructive behaviors. As a result, we learn to meet our life rather than avoid it. The fruits of the first shift are openness and resilience.

The second shift is from, What can I learn about myself? to, What can I discover about my relationships with others? This is the beginning of turning away from self-centered thought. The fruits of the second shift are empathy and authentic compassion.

The third shift is waking up to a reality without boundaries. We recognize that we are all in this together. We begin to experience the world as it actually is. The fruit of the third shift is a deep composure that arises from clear-seeing.

In 1967, Pete Townshend of The Who wrote the hit song "I Can See for Miles." To date it remains their biggest hit. The song was rarely performed live because both the vocals and the percussion were too complex to replicate on stage.

Townshend had just emerged from an LSD trip when he wrote the song. In it, he talks about his sadness and heartache. While doing acid, however, he experienced a great spaciousness and a deep quiet. When I listen to the lyrics, I understand that he didn't avoid his sadness—he immersed himself in it. Suddenly the dense emotional fog dissolved and he could see beyond his small, suffering ego-self "for miles and miles and miles."

But Townshend's chemically induced experience of forgetting the self and identifying with all life was unsustainable because the second shift—compassion for others—was left out. His behavior afterward didn't change. Even so, the experience created a huge footprint in his life. About a year later, Townshend swore off drugs and began a sincere meditation practice.

DOING THE WORK

1. Think about a time you experienced failure of one type or another. What did you learn from this chapter that could help you to benefit from that failure?

2. Think about something you are trying to do well. Notice how you're talking to yourself about it; notice the labels you use to

judge your performance. Try replacing these labels with this question: Am I making my best effort? Practice this daily for two or three weeks. Do you notice a change in your attitude?

3. In this chapter, I suggested that learning to fail skillfully involves renunciation. Consider the relationship between renunciation and self-acceptance. Are they mutually exclusive behaviors? Or are they like the nuanced and complementary movements of dance? Think about a specific area of your life where these two qualities are already alive and dancing together.

4. Recall the story about the samurai who wanted to become a Zen monk. When he asked the master, "How long can I carry my sword?" the master replied, "as long as you can." What does this story say about self-acceptance? Do you agree or disagree with the Zen master? Why or why not?

PART TWO

Suturing and Healing

SIX

The Wisdom of Humility

In the age when life on earth was full, no one paid any special attention to worthy men, nor did they single out the man of ability. Rulers were simply the highest branches on the tree, and the people were like deer in the woods. They were honest and righteous without realizing they were "doing their duty." They loved each other and did not know this was "love of neighbor." They deceived no one yet they did not know they were "men to be trusted." They were reliable but did not know this was "good faith." They lived freely together giving and taking, and did not know they were generous. For this reason their deeds have not been narrated. They made no history.

—ZHUANGZI

ZHUANGZI WAS A PHILOSOPHER and writer who lived around the fourth century B.C.E. He used parables, allegories, and paradox to describe the way of being in the world that became the foundation of Taoism. Zhuangzi believed that when human activity was aligned with the natural world, there would be harmony.

Rather than thinking about nature as something to be mastered, the Taoists look toward nature as their teacher. Nature is infinitely wise and infinitely complex, and the only way to approach it is with humility.

NATURAL HUMILITY

Humility comes from the Latin root *humus*, meaning "earth" or "ground." In English, humus means soil. Human beings came from the salt water of the oceans and from the richness of the soil. The philosopher and author Alan Watts used to say that the earth is "peopling"—producing human beings the way an apple tree "apples" by producing fruit.

The humus is aerated and moist because it's not separate from the air and rain. It supports us, but not in the way we're accustomed to think. It consists of fire, air, water, and all manner of decomposing beings. When you sink all the way into the humus, beautiful wildflowers can bloom right where you are.

But there's no security in being a wildflower. It feels much safer to be a polished stone, to look good to others and stand out in the world. But very little grows on a polished stone. Besides, if you think about it, you may realize that you've been stony for too many years already. Try something different, sink down to the earth. All the nourishment you need is there.

With natural humility, you go all the way down into the humus rather than sticking up like you're some big deal because you've got something that others don't have. When you sink all the way to the ground, you actually *are* a big deal—not because you are you, but because you are *not* you. You've touched the ground of all being, which is not a solid ground at all. It is completely aerated with all life.

Instead of trying to be somebody special, inhabiting a natural humility allows you to be something much more. It allows you the freedom to be nobody in particular. Nobody to defend or uphold, nobody to judge good or bad, and no one in need of redemption.

HUMILITY AND SELF-RESPECT

Suzuki Roshi had a unique take on self-respect. He said, "When you do something without thinking about doing something, that is self-respect." He was not talking about the kind of respect that emanates *from* you *to* you. True self-respect is bigger than that; it is bigger than the small self that is always seeking respect. Respectfulness is an abiding quality that arises naturally from a feeling of interconnectedness. It includes you, but also everything else.

When I was a student at Stanford, Suzuki asked me to start a sitting group there. He committed to coming once a week to sit with us, and I managed to find a room for the morning sittings in the home of a few grad students. While we sat, the grad students slept.

The house was always a mess. So every week, immediately after the sitting, Suzuki jumped up and started cleaning. And of course, we were expected to help.

But we didn't want to help. Housekeeping was nobody work. We were Stanford students; we were striving to be somebody. We had classes to attend, papers to write, and teachers to impress. When I explained to Suzuki how busy we were, he was very sympathetic, but not in the way I had hoped. "Oh," he said. "Then we should start an hour earlier."

Suzuki had an interesting way of thinking about cleaning. He would say, "When you sweep the floor, just sweep." I started out feeling that sweeping the floor was a chore. I did it with a heavy attitude. But then I saw how lightly Suzuki went about it. Eventually I began to experience some lightness also. I saw how sweeping the floor can be just like meditation if you give yourself to it. I noticed how the broom felt in my hands and the color of the floor, and I felt the movement of my body. The grumbling dropped away.

Suzuki showed us how to bring our meditative mind off the cushion and into our life. What good is it if it doesn't infiltrate your whole life?

Every week, I watched Suzuki ground himself in each activity. He didn't separate the important from the menial. He showed how any activity becomes enlightened activity if we just give ourselves to it. After a while, working alongside him became just as wonderful as sitting zazen (Zen meditation) with him. There was no difference.

The kind of natural humility Suzuki manifested is the basis for true self-respect. It is not something you can pursue. It is not something you can possess or gain through your effort. If you think you have it, then already you have separated from it.

We can stop using life to validate me, me, me. Self-respect arises naturally when we stop seeing life as a tool that either sustains or endangers us.

HUMILITY AND AUTHENTICITY

> We walk the path that no one has trod, following the footprints left by others.
>
> —ZEN PROVERB

Chinese Zen master Gutei lived in the ninth century. He lived a solitary life so he could focus one-pointedly on his practice. He thought his understanding of the dharma could measure up to any test.

One day, as he was meditating, a mysterious woman showed up, drifting like a warm breeze into his hut. She circled him three times and then said, "If you can say a turning word, I will take off my hat." This meant she would stay.

Gutei really wanted this mysterious woman to stay. But he froze. So she left.

A turning word could be anything—a phrase, a gesture, even silence—so long as it bubbles up freshly from an open heart. In his heart, Master Gutei wanted the woman to stay. So why didn't he just ask her to stay? Or offer her a cup of tea? Or blush foolishly like an eight-year-old because his heart was turning cartwheels? After all, authenticity was all she was asking for.

When we are not *trying* to be authentic, we do not fall into confusion when life unfolds in unexpected ways. All that night, Gutei tossed and turned, saying over and over to himself, "You stupid fellow. You stupid fellow."

There are moments that challenge us to open more fully to life, to adapt, to be pliable, to engage life on new levels. That means going beyond our comfort zone. It means giving up the idea of being true to who we think we are.

When I was a young man studying with Katagiri Roshi at MZMC, I went to Naropa University in Colorado to study Buddhism. When I returned, Katagiri said, "Now that you have studied Buddhism, it is time for you to teach it."

Public speaking was way beyond my comfort zone. If he had told me before I left that I would have to teach when I got back, I wouldn't have gone. But I did it anyway, because my teacher asked me to.

Most learning begins with behavior that feels awkward and unnatural. You can stick with learned behaviors you already have in order to be "true to yourself." But this is a very small, restricted self, one that is not flexible and available to Big Life.

I had a friend I'll call Rachel. She was conscientious and humble. When she got a promotion at work, it felt natural for her to disclose her insecurity about her new position. She told everyone, "Oh, I don't know about this new job. I'm having all sorts of problems." She truly felt that she was just being authentic. But soon her subordinates became demoralized. It isn't surprising, is it? They weren't being supported by her, because she was too caught up in her own insecurity.

Rachel fits our standard idea of humility. Her story is a good example of how confused many of us are about humility and authenticity. Hers was not deep humility. She was not being nobody. She was a well-defined *someone* who was caught in her ideas about who she was and what she was capable of.

Authenticity can be an excuse for sticking with what is comfortable, for sticking to "who we are." But true authenticity is not about sticking to our conditioned ideas about ourselves.

Suzuki Roshi came to this country in his fifties, and he thrived here because in his humility he was free to do what he wanted to do. When his student Trudy Dixon was suffering from cancer, she invited Suzuki to visit her family ranch in Montana. On his return, I picked him up from the airport. When I asked him about his trip, he began to tell me about going horseback riding with Trudy.

I said, "I didn't know you knew how to ride a horse."

"No," he exclaimed. "I don't know. But the horse knew."

When Suzuki's student Betty was suffering from depression, she couldn't bear to come to the zendo (meditation hall). But she loved to play to tennis. So she invited Suzuki to play tennis. I happened to come across him as he was leaving for the court, wearing shorts and a sailor's hat to cover his bald head.

I said, "I didn't know you knew how to play tennis."

"I don't," he said, "but Betty knows."

I asked if I could come along and watch. It was a riot. They only played about fifteen minutes, but they had a good time together.

Suzuki wasn't limited by a self-image that dictated what he could and couldn't do. Authenticity that is aerated with humility includes flexibility. Maybe there is no one authentic self. Maybe we are a collage of selves, and we can try on different ones. Rather than "working on ourselves" all the time, spending years with a therapist, self-help books, and seminars about personal growth, how about adopting a playful attitude toward your collage of selves?

But it's not even *your* collage. It's a collage of experiences that are always changing, so there's nothing to grasp on to and say, "This is me—this is who I am." So, please, enjoy your story, but don't stick to it. It's just one story among many that are always bubbling up.

What is identity, anyway? Isn't it an appropriation of the past that we glom on to and project into the future? With authenticity that is aerated with humility, you can step out of the shadow of your past and stretch the limits of who you are. You don't have to become entranced by a single story line.

Václav Havel served as the last president of Czechoslovakia and, from 1993 to 2003, the first president of the Czech Republic after the Czech-Slovak split. In his earlier life he had been a lab assistant, a stagehand, a dramatist, a moral philosopher, and a political prisoner for forty years. He tried on a multiplicity of selves, didn't he? And he was humble. Here is a delightful excerpt from the December 1, 2014, issue of the *New Yorker* entitled "Havel in Jerusalem," by David Remnick:

> Not long after his unlikely rise from Czech prisoner to Czech President, Václav Havel paid a visit to Moscow. Until that moment, the leaders of Eastern and Central Europe had arrived at the gates of the Kremlin as little more than nerve-racked supplicants. They came to receive instructions and to pay obeisance to the General Secretary. Now Havel was there to see Mikhail Gorbachev, but, with an air of modest self-confidence, he carried a set of demands and an ironic prop. As Michael

Žantovský tells the story in his excellent new biography, Havel asked that the Soviet Union remove its troops from Czech territory, and that the two nations sign a statement declaring them equals. Gorbachev, who had already relinquished his imperial holdings, agreed, at which point Havel produced a peace pipe, telling Gorbachev that it had been given to him by the chief of a Native American tribe during a recent trip to the United States. "Mr. President," Havel said, "it occurred to me right there and then that I should bring this pipe to Moscow and that the two of us should smoke it together." Žantovský, who was Havel's press aide at the time, recalls that Gorbachev "looked at the pipe as if it were a hand grenade." Then the Soviet leader turned to Havel and stammered, "But I . . . don't smoke."

What happened to the charismatic Soviet leader at that moment? Why did something as humble and earthy as a Native American peace pipe throw him off his game? I wonder if he lay awake that night, as Zen master Gutei did, saying to himself, "You stupid fellow, you stupid fellow."

The political careers of President Gorbachev and President Havel had many parallels. Like Havel, Gorbachev served as his country's last General Secretary of the Communist Party and then as the first elected president of the Soviet Union after a major restructuring. Other world leaders described both men as warm, personable, and charismatic. But Havel had something Gorbachev lacked: the kind of authentic flexibility and earthy composure that arises from natural humility. He had been steeping in the humus his entire life.

I am the kind of person who would not be in the least surprised if, in the very middle of my Presidency, I were to be summoned and led off to stand trial before some shadowy tribunal, or taken straight to a quarry. . . . Nor would I be surprised if I were to suddenly hear the reveille and wake up in my prison cell, and then, with great bemusement, proceed to tell my fellow prisoners everything that had happened to me in the past six months. . . . The lower I am, the more proper my place seems; and the higher I am, the stronger my suspicion that there has been some mistake.

—VÁCLAV HAVEL

HUMILITY AND CONFIDENCE

Humility and confidence are two sides of the same coin. The more naturally humble you are, the more confident you are. It requires confidence to simply be, without trying to present a persona that others will respect or admire, without posturing or pretense, without the need to be right all the time. If you worry about being right, then you have a very fragile confidence. But with humility your confidence becomes steady. It can withstand turbulent times when things don't go the way you thought they would. It is not an arrogant, adolescent confidence based on some accomplishment that you are proud of.

Confidence aerated with humility is light and buoyant. When you fall down, you just get up. Falling down is no problem. Asking for help is no problem. Confidence without humility is so heavy it's hard to get up when you've fallen—it tells you that failure means you can't do it. You're embarrassed and even ashamed to ask for help because that means you're not good enough. Confidence without humility is rigid. It breaks easily because it is clinging to a specific self-image.

Confidence that arises from humility doesn't depend on accomplishment because it is the parent of accomplishment—not the child of it. We strive to do our best without comparing our wins against the accomplishments of others, because our confidence is not shored up by others.

When we strive without judging and comparing, we naturally lift others up with us. You don't have to strive to be a leader because you are lifted naturally and organically to a position of leadership. You know how to lead without separating yourself from those you are leading. You are with them, really listening to them, knowing them, supporting them, and being supported by them. That is the kind of confidence that Václav Havel embodied. That is what true confidence is about.

So far, we have discussed three qualities that arise from natural humility: authenticity, self-respect, and confidence. As human beings, humility may be our greatest natural resource, which is the key to unlocking the wisdom of humility.

> KEY #6: Natural humility is the source of
> authenticity, self-respect, and confidence.

When you are grounded in these three qualities, there arises the possibility of experiencing an altered state that is both magical and natural. It is perhaps the deepest and most connected state that human beings can experience.

HUMILITY AND FLOW

Our evolutionary coping mechanism, the fear response—fight, flight, freeze—has outlived its usefulness for most situations that we face. It has become the problem rather the solution. It evolved to protect the body, but our body is rarely in danger in this modern world. Now the fear response is mostly about protecting our self-image.

We have another mechanism that may be even more deeply

rooted than the fight, flight, or freeze response. It allows us to thrive in a complex world. Most commonly it is called the *flow state*. If you're a runner, you may know it as "runner's high." If you're into team sports, you may call it "being in the zone." If you're a jazz musician, it's "in the pocket." If you're an activist or caretaker, you may have experienced "helper's high." If you're a Taoist, you may call it "riding the clouds and following the wind."

Like fight/flight/freeze, a flow state arises unbidden. We can't command it, but we can create the conditions for it. In sports, Michael Jordan is a great example of someone who knew how to promote a flow state. There was a certain quality of mind that Jordan brought to the basketball court. He concentrated on the ball and his moves, not the crowd or even his opponents. He was immersed in the intrinsic pleasure of the game itself.

I call the kind of deep concentration Jordan brought to the court *bare awareness*. (Others call it *mindfulness*.) With bare awareness, you don't get stuck on a goal. You're not trying to achieve something through your concentration.

When Jordan went into a flow state, he seemed to control the whole court. Even those watching in the stands and from their living rooms participated in his flow state. In those moments we were able to suspend our judgments and concerns and become a participant in the wonderful, synchronous activity unfolding on the court. Who is really the center if everyone together is in flow? It's a multi-centered flow.

The term *flow* was coined by Mihaly Csikszentmihalyi in his seminal work, *Flow: The Psychology of Optimal Experience*, published in 1990. Here's how he described flow in an interview in *Wired* magazine:

[Flow is] being completely involved in an activity for its own sake. The ego falls away. Time flies. Every action, movement, and thought follows inevitably from the previous one, like playing jazz. Your whole being is involved, and you're using your skills to the utmost.

There are as many descriptions of flow as there are people who have experienced it. But there seem to be three components that are central to all the accounts: a sense of timelessness, effortlessness, and selflessness.

Timelessness. Many describe their experience of flow as one in which time slows down or stops. For others, time speeds up—hours pass by in what seem like minutes. But actually, a flow state is beyond time. In a flow state, we get a taste of the timeless nature of reality.

Effortlessness. Of all the descriptions of flow, I think the Taoists described it best. They called it *wu wei,* meaning the action of non-action, doing non-doing, or effortless effort. Wu wei is a deep but seemingly effortless engagement in an activity. But it is effortless effort. Effort is involved, but it doesn't feel like effort because it doesn't involve exertion. Like a river flowing north or a wave rising toward the sky, with effortless effort we are in complete alignment with the flow of things. Wu wei is only possible when we can get the self out of the way—in other words, when we are nobody.

Selflessness. When we say no-self, we are not denying our existence as individuals. We are confirming our existence as more, as beyond, as both individual and undivided. In a flow state, we get a taste of our undivided nature. Awareness and activity merge. The doer and the deed are inseparable.

No one walks this path
this autumn night.

—BASHO

Since Csikszentmihalyi published *Flow* in 1990, a lot of research has focused on activities that promote flow. It turns out that flow states triggered by altruistic activity have been known to last the longest. I think of flow as a form of enlightened activity because it's a direct experience of interconnectedness manifesting as deep synchronicity. We don't experience it very often, because flow involves letting go of the subject/object dichotomy that governs ordinary thinking.

If you really want to experience flow take some advice from the Taoists. They have been telling us how to enter flow states for twenty-five hundred years.

> Flow with whatever is happening and let your mind be free.
> Stay centered by accepting whatever you are doing.
> This is the ultimate.
>
> —ZHUANGZI

DOING THE WORK

1. Consider Suzuki Roshi's comment, "When you do something without thinking about doing something, that is self-respect." How does this approach to self-respect compare to your own approach? What, if any, are the downsides of taking his advice too literally?

2. The thirteenth-century Japanese Zen master Dogen commented in one of his later writings that his life had consisted of "mistake after mistake." Yet there is no hint of self-reproach or self-recrimination in his writing or teaching. Based on your own experience, how do these fit together?

SEVEN

Suturing What
Was Rent Asunder

SUTURING WHAT WAS RENT ASUNDER is about
healing the gap between ourselves and others
caused by an unnatural feeling of separation. For twenty-five
hundred years Buddhists have used meditation to heal the gap.
For Taoists, nature does the job. In Zen, we use both.

A major difference between suturing and flow is that with
suturing we may not even realize it's happening. Suturing is like
walking through mist: you don't realize you're getting wet until
you're soaked all the way through.

There are two approaches to healing the gap: through *self-
power* and through *other-power*. So far, we have focused on self-
power. Through our own efforts, we systematically deconstruct
our conditioned ideas about worthiness, money, sex, failure, and
humility, and open ourselves up to a fresh approach to life.

This chapter focuses on the other-power approach, the healing
power of nature.

When I was five years old, my family lived in a small house on a hill that overlooked the San Francisco Bay. There was a place behind our house that my parents didn't want me to know about. If you stood in a certain spot, you could see the entire bay, but it was off-limits because my parents felt it was unsafe. What my parents didn't know was that I *did* know about it. And I wanted to see it.

Early one morning, before anyone else woke up, I snuck out of the house and went there. I'll never forget the experience. As I looked down at the vast expanse of water, I didn't feel small anymore. I didn't feel lonely living on that hill with no one to play with. I felt full, completely full—and completely empty at the same time.

Years later, when I was sixteen and in a deep state of depression, the memory of how I'd felt that day as a five-year-old drew me back to the overlook. I wanted to recapture the healing experience, though at the time I didn't think of it as healing. I just remembered the joy, the wonder, and the feeling that I was part of something huge.

MEDITATING ON THE NATURAL WORLD

For years I have practiced and taught two types of meditation: a mountain meditation and a water meditation. In the mountain meditation, we experience our natural capacity to be steady and upright, even as life flows through and around us. In the water meditation, we experience the ever-changing fluidity of all that arises.

In the mountain meditation, you sit in a strong, upright position. When you identify with the mountain, you are unmovable, imperturbable. The mountain is not bothered by the comings and goings of clouds, birds, rain, or snow. It doesn't reject or attach to life's passing expressions and manifestations. As you consciously identify with the mountain, you may come to feel an imperturbable, unshakable calmness.

In the water mediation, you lie down in a comfortable position. You let your breath flow in and out and you let your thoughts flow in and out, noticing the contours of your body and where your skin touches the bed or the floor, and the contours and textures of the steady flow of thoughts and sensations arising, peaking, and then dissolving. When everything is flowing, the gap between your awareness and the object of your awareness begins to close.

In the water meditation, you're so empty of self that all life flows through you, giving you everything you need. Water washes everything away. Even the mountain is flowing. If the mountain doesn't know that it's flowing, or in other words, if it tries to resist its own nature by remaining static, then it will soon flow pretty fast, because a mountain includes erosion from inside by geothermal activity and from outside by rivers, rain, and wind.

Walking meditation is another good way to connect with the natural world. A warm summer breeze shows us how to let go of our worries and concerns. Sure, our worries will come back— but there's always more breeze. It's only our clinginess that divides us from our completeness just as we are. Without clinging to passing thoughts, we are naturally free and unhindered in our activities. It can be as easy as putting one foot in front of the other.

THE MOUNTAINS AND WATERS SUTRA

The root word for *suture* means "to thread [something] together." The related Sanskrit word *sutra* refers to Buddhist scriptures. A sutra is a source of healing. Its purpose is to suture together something that's been split, some hurt we have, a feeling of separation, alienation, or isolation from the world around us.

In a sutra, the suturing is usually done through the wisdom of our ancestors. But the Mountains and Waters Sutra, written by the Zen master Dogen, speaks of another kind of wisdom. We are surrounded by the sutra, under our feet, overhead, and inside us. So there is nothing to read, nothing to understand, and nothing to do. The suturing is done by the mountains and waters: nature itself is the source of healing.

Although Dogen is writing about mountains, his intention is not to teach about mountains and waters. Mountains and waters *are* the sutra—they suture through their very beingness. They show us how to experience our primal sense of connectedness as we intimately experience each sight and sound without being caught by our thoughts about them.

Dogen's Mountains and Waters Sutra is the earth, the trees, and the underbrush of the mountain; it's the lakes, the streams, and the rivers. Many of us notice a deep happiness or an unexpected calm when we're close to nature. When we spend contemplative time by mountains and water, our sense of separation, anxiety, and loneliness abates, and what has been torn asunder gradually begins to heal. The healing happens naturally if we are open to it—one breath, one stitch; one stitch, one breath.

The breeze from the mountain, the breeze from the lake, the breeze from each out-breath and in-breath heals the wound so we can return to our original wholeness, our original completeness. New anxieties and fears may arise to sever our feeling of interconnectedness, but there's always another breeze, always another breath, to suture these new wounds.

Dogen uses language as ungraspable as mountains and waters themselves. If you try to get your mind around the Sutra, you'll be lost. How about just letting Dogen's words flow through you, without trying to figure them out?

Mountains walking is just like humans walking.
To understand mountains walking is to understand your
  own walking.
If you know your own walking you know the walking of
  mountains.

Pause for a moment and look down at your own body. It will tell you about the immediate present, which is always changing, always walking. Even if you're sitting or lying down, what you experience as a self is a continuously shifting kaleidoscope of forms, patterns, sensations, mental images, thoughts, desires, and memories; and yet you are sitting perfectly still, like a mountain.

For many years, I've gone to the Caribbean every winter with my family. There's a mountain right outside the kitchen window of our house on the island. By most standards, it's not really a mountain; actually, it's barely a hill. But that's okay; it doesn't know.

When I look with my small, tired mind, it's just a hill. But if I look with my fresh mind, which is no mind at all, it's never the same. Sometimes, I see its vividness. Other times, its colors appear faded, pale, and washed out. Often, it is shrouded in mist and seems a little mysterious. This, I think, is what Dogen meant when he wrote that a mountain's walking is no different from a human's walking.

This body-mind that I inhabit was named Morris Timothy when it was born seventy-three years ago. And then it was just Tim, and no longer Morris Timothy. Years later, when I was the smallest kid in school, it was no longer just Tim but Tiny Tim, which this body-mind hated. Then Daddy. When I was ordained as a Zen priest, it became Zentetsu. And then Grandpa.

Our identities and roles change like the seasons. The mountain does not cling to summer as the trees lose their leaves and the lakes begin to freeze, nor to winter as the snow melts. The less we identify with a particular role, the freer we become. The mountain can teach you about a freedom that is more fundamental than the roles that limit our movement and imagination.

When we study our own walking we should study forward walking and backward walking.

—DOGEN

If you want to understand something, "take the backward step and shine your light of awareness inward." Whenever you are anxious or stressed out about something, take a backward step and inquire into it. Trace it back to its root. Anxiety and the obsessive thoughts that come with it say that I am here and you are there, and can make you feel closed off and isolated. When you trace your anxiety back to its root, your sense of separation and isolation subsides. As we stitch together what was rent asunder, we begin to experience this great life as a dance.

As I'm writing this, it is winter here in Minnesota. Across from the Zen center is Lake Bde Maka Ska, which used to be called Lake Calhoun. Its surface is a thick layer of ice. Every year around this time, I begin to yearn for spring when life returns to Minnesota. The other day, the ice looked as if it was about to break up. Immediately I began to anticipate spring, trying to ignore the last vestiges of winter.

The you that spends so much time regretting the past, avoiding the present, and rehearsing for the future is just surface ice that distances you from yourself and from what actually is. Even as we yearn to experience the vitality of life, we cling to the ice because it feels safe and reliable. Yet in our bones we know this isn't true. Life is messy and unpredictable. The ego shell is just surface ice. It offers a veneer of solidity and stability, so we cling to it for protection.

In meditation, we begin to see that even the ice is part of the changing seasons. In winter, during the dark times, the lake becomes covered with a layer of protective ice, but down below the water still flows. The water is always flowing, even in our darkest moments when it seems that ice is all there is. Our heart may ache, but it keeps beating, our blood continues to flow, sensations undulate, emotions arise and fade away, moods come and go. Spring comes, and winter's ice melts.

> KEY #7: When you're sutured, life
> becomes lighter and more transparent.

We are always being supported by the energy and vitality that surrounds and penetrates all things. As you allow the ice to dissolve into the water, the roles you identify with become more fluid. You can move from one to another without becoming confused or overwhelmed. This is what Dogen called "riding the clouds and following the wind."

Once when I was visiting Green Gulch Farm Zen Center in Muir Beach, California, I came across Reb Anderson, a well-known teacher and author. He was walking along a path toward the ocean to go swimming. Well, this was September, and the Pacific in September is quite cold. I asked Reb if he would be wearing a wet suit.

"No," he said. "I've gotten used to the water."

So is it possible to get used to this great ocean of life and just dive into it without a wet suit? With nothing separating us from it, even though the water is cold and rough sometimes?

The wet suit separates us from the energy of life. Can we open our pores and experience it just as it is?

I think so.

I think so.

When we study our own walking, we should use numerous worlds as our standards.

If we only rely on our own concepts and beliefs, our world is too small. We get stuck. We become rigid. If you really want to understand life, whether it's your own life or your lover's life or your neighbor's life, you can't be attached to your own standards.

By the standards of the ancient sages, all that exists—sentient and non-sentient, seen and unseen, conscious and unconscious—is composed of four basic elements: earth, water, air, and fire. The early Greeks formalized this view into a scientific model that described the properties and behavior of matter. In many ways, it is still referred to today.

The earth element is heavy, solid, and fixed in nature. It separates things and makes them discrete. We feel grounded by the earth, and it draws us toward it. Earth retains, solidifies, coagulates, condenses, sustains, supports, and endures. Seasonally, it is related to fall or autumn. In the fall, things return to the humus and the fertilization of new life begins.

Water is the source of all life. It is the most passive and most receptive of the four elements and the greatest receiver and absorber of energy. It dissolves, cleanses, purifies, fertilizes, and germinates. It corresponds to winter.

Air, being the most refined and mutable of the elements, allows for movement, contact, and exchange. It is related to spring.

Fire is the most active, energetic, and volatile element. It refines, distills, and transforms and is the greatest emitter of energy. Its seasonal correlate is summer.

By the standards of shamanic traditions, suturing means bringing the rhythms and patterns of our lives into harmony with nature. Along with the four elements and four seasons, the shamans also integrated the four cardinal directions and four personality types, or archetypes.

From the east, which is the direction of the rising sun, comes spring. It correlates to the element of air. Illumination and inspiration come from the east, and the corresponding personality type is the teacher. When we look toward the east, we see things in a new light and gain fresh perspectives.

South is summertime, and the corresponding element is fire. From the south come ritual and celebration, through singing, dancing, and sharing. From the east, we have gained insight and understanding; in the south, we share that understanding. It is here that we learn the lessons of the full, clear, open, and strong heart. From the south comes the archetype of the visionary.

The west brings autumn and the element of water. To face west is to turn our attention inward. It is time for recognizing the conditioned patterns that rule our lives and for freeing ourselves from them. From the west come spiritual freedom and the archetype of the healer.

North is the direction of winter and the element of earth. According to the shamanic tradition, north is the place where we return to the Great Mystery. Facing northward, we empty ourselves out so we can receive the wisdom of our true nature. It correlates to the archetype of the inner warrior.

I have been very fortunate in my life to work and practice for two decades with two Zen teachers, Suzuki Roshi and Katagiri Roshi. In my mid-forties, I also worked for several years with two shamanic teachers, Michael Harner and Elmer Running. On several occasions, I spent twenty-four hours or so immersed in nature doing solitary contemplation.

Once, my friend Paul and I decided to do a formal Lakota vision quest, a *hanbleceya*. Elmer agreed to be our guide. Paul and I drove to the Rosebud Indian Reservation in South Dakota where

Elmer lived. He and his wife had a stretch of land that they'd turned into an oasis of sorts, with sweats, late-night healing ceremonies, and hanbleceyas held regularly, led by Elmer.

A hanbleceya begins with a traditional Lakota sweat. Paul, Elmer, myself, and several members from the Lakota reservation sat in a circle inside a small-frame structure covered with animal skins and blankets. It was less than five feet high.

A Lakota sweat takes place around a fire pit filled with stones that have been heated until they are glowing. It is pitch dark; all you can see is the glow from the rocks. The sweat is about prayer. We prayed to *Tunkashila*, Grandfather Rock. The Lakota believe that rocks are the oldest and most fundamental form of the ancient earth element. So in the sweat, we asked Grandfather Rock to support us during the five-day hanbleceya.

As we prayed, Elmer poured water over the stones, creating steam and making the rocks glow even brighter. Steam engulfed the lodge. It was so hot we had to hunker down to avoid getting burned.

Afterward, Elmer drove Paul and me to the top of two separate hills. I was dropped off first. Elmer marked off a small circle, then left me in my underwear, with only a pipe and a blanket. He drove Paul to another hill and repeated the ritual. For the next five days, we were alone in our small circles with only the four elements to sustain us. No food, water, or clothes. Only a pipe filled with tobacco. We had strict instructions to hold the pipe gently in our hands, day and night, and take care that no grains of the tobacco fell out of the bowl.

The pipe was made of a very hard, red rock quarried in Pipestone, Minnesota. The Lakota have been making their sacred pipes from pipestone for centuries. This one was especially revered because the pipestone was red—red because of the blood of their ancestors, congealed by their deep suffering. So during the hanbleceya, we received the support of the Lakota ancestors, whose trials and tribulations solidified into the determination, strength, and stability required to move beyond suffering.

The tobacco represented all our relatives, which, for the Lakota people, include all beings, sentient and non-sentient. Every grain is sacred and cannot be spilled because each represents a different species of being. The bowl containing the tobacco was round, symbolizing the circle of life.

I slept with the pipe resting on my chest. Once, it slid off and a few grains fell out. Feeling around in the dark, I gently picked up each one and returned it to the bowl of the pipe.

After five days, Elmer picked us up and drove us back to the sweat lodge for a second sweat.

On my way up to the hill, Elmer had urged me to empty myself and continually pray for help and support from the world beyond. Now, on the way down, he asked, "Did you see one of them spirit eagles?"

"Yes," I replied. "It was wonderful."

He looked at me pointedly and said, "A lot of people see them, but few live out what they were shown."

When the eagle enters someone's life, she offers two gifts. Her eagle eyes see the smallest mouse from a great distance, clearly distinguishing it from everything else. Her gift to an initiate is the ability to live effectively in the world, seeing the specific needs and concerns of each individual.

The second gift involves the eagle's great wingspan. As she flies higher and higher, she sees all life as one undivided whole. Entering the life of an initiate, she offers the ability to act from a feeling of wholeness.

During our exit sweat, our pipes were lit. As each piece of tobacco heated up, it melded into all the others. All the species of the world were returning to their original oneness. In the first sweat, the center glow had been all we could see. In the exit sweat, we could also see the redness from the burning tobacco as it moved around the circle, passed from hand to hand. We smoked the tobacco until there was no trace of separation between any of the bits of tobacco, any of the four elements, or any of us. The essence of all that exists was contained in the smoke. What was once individual was now undivided.

After the sweat, Paul and I cooked a big meal for everyone with food we had brought with us. The meal was intended to show our appreciation for their support. They'd all been praying for us during our vision quest on the mountain. There were about fifteen to twenty people there. Then it was time for Paul and me to share stories about our five-day ordeal.

What was the point of this experience? For me, a hanbleceya is very much like a Zen retreat. It involves a continual emptying out of the self so we can go beyond it, and can tap into our undivided nature. In retreats, as in a hanbleceya, we are brought up against the edge of our ego. We experience the fragility of the ice and know that it isn't enough to support and sustain us.

For nothing can be sole or whole
That has not been rent.

—W. B. YEATS

SUTURING THE ORIGINAL WOUND

We sit together, the mountain and me, until only the mountain remains.

—RYOKAN

My parents loved hiking the Sierra Nevada. When I was nine, they decided I was old enough to make it to the 14,000-foot peak of

Mount Langley in eastern California. We started out from Golden Trout Camp before dawn. I remember wondering that morning how I would ever make it to the top. To help ease my mind, my parents gave me a map of the trail. It became my lifeline. I trusted that it would lead us to the top and back down again.

But it didn't get us to the top. When we reached the timberline, the map ended. There were no more landmarks for me to look toward and mark off as we passed them by. I was scared. No longer did I experience the comfort of hiking through forested hills with the reassurance of my map. Instead, there was nothing but barren rocks and an occasional stunted tree as far as the eye could see.

We often have the same experience in a spiritual practice. We've learned some basic meditation techniques, but at some point, we have to let go of them if we are going to move beyond our familiar patterns of being into the vast unknown.

My mother stayed just far enough ahead of me to stay within sight—just as an accomplished spiritual teacher does. If I had lagged too far behind, I would have lost sight of her. So I kept moving—one breath, one step, one step, one breath—until finally we reached the top.

My parents wanted me to sign the book fastened to a large rock. They thought it would make up for the long ordeal of the climb.

But I wasn't interested in signing my name. I was immersed in the wonder of the mountain range that I was surrounded by: mountain after mountain under a cloudless blue sky. My fear was gone, transformed into a joyous feeling of spaciousness, a feeling I would experience many more times in my life through my meditation practice.

Before fear can be transformed into joy, we have to learn to endure it. We have to come to know it intimately, to endure it, and eventually cultivate a relationship with it. That is what was happening as I climbed Mount Langley. Without first being rent, the suturing that I experienced on the peak could not have happened.

The mountain had a lot to teach me that day. If you can take the first step, you can take the last one. During a meditation retreat, if you can take the first breath, you can take the last one. Each step on the mountain, each breath in a retreat, is just like the first. Between the first and the last, maybe you have to stop and rest.

So stop and rest.

Maybe you will experience some fear. Fear is not bad. There are times when you should be afraid. Being afraid is no problem if there's no confusion in it.

Whatever your companion—fear, frustration, joy, boredom, or rapture—still, each step is identical to the first. One foot is in the air; the other foot is grounded. One inhale, one exhale. One forward-moving foot, one stabilizing foot. Simple. It's very simple. It's only your mind showing you movies that makes it feel difficult. This is what Mount Langley taught me that day. It was my first truly terrible experience that became something wonderful.

Our preoccupation with thoughts and concepts stifles our sense of curiosity, buoyancy, and deep joy as our lives unfold. Like the mountains and waters, our natural stability and fluidity were there before the appearance of thoughts and concepts. Before we were born, we were riding the clouds and soaring in the wind, naturally free and unhindered in our activities—and at the same time solidly rooted in rich earth right below us.

I'm not talking about religious ideas about reincarnation or being reborn; I'm talking about something deeper than that.

Suturing, on the deepest and most primal level, is about the birth wound, our initial experience of separation. It is about discovering that we are still in the womb, completely supported by it, because the womb is the entire universe. Suturing our original wound comes unbidden, and often from ordinary, everyday activities.

Here is an experience one of my students shared with me:

> The lawn in front of the house where I grew up was spacious and uneven. In winter, mounds of snow piled up where the driveway and sidewalk met the grass. In spring, snowmelt settled in the dip in the lawn, making a puddle the size of a pond. One day, when I was seven or eight years old, I noticed that the water in the puddle reflected the clouds and the treetops in the sky. The sight of it drew me in to the puddle, and I stepped gingerly, not to ruffle its mirror surface. Suddenly, I was walking not on the ground but among the treetops and the clouds, on blue sky. It was as if something shifted in my brain and opened the top of my head. I felt light and free.
>
> One morning sixty years later, I was in the garden at the Minnesota Zen Meditation Center for walking meditation. The garden in summer is lush with foliage and flowers in bloom. A stone path wends around a huge oak tree. It edges spikes of bracken fern and broad-leafed elephant ears among smaller bishop's-weed and baby tears. On this particular day, the larger leaves were sprinkled with dewdrops bright as diamonds. My gaze fell on an elephant ear with a single dewdrop at its tip. In the dewdrop, I saw the leafy treetop and the dawning daylight of the sky.

DOING THE WORK

Mountain Meditation: Sitting in Nature. Begin with a calming and centering meditation like the one described in chapter one. Check your posture: is it strong and upright, like a mountain?

Gather your attention into bare awareness. No inside, no outside, just the light of your awareness shining on everything. When you are ready, allow yourself to contemplate the mountain, to arouse within you the felt-sense of steadiness, stability, and balance.

Whatever is going on, the mountain is not bothered: the mountain just sits. When the sun shines down, the mountain just sits. A storm whips up with strong winds and driving rain and the mountain is not bothered; it just sits.

Scarred by trails, roads, and lumberjacks, the mountain just sits—not bothered by the comings and goings of things and events. Just sitting. Just being. Hikers pass by, building fires and jabbering away night and day—the mountain just sits, not resisting or contracting, not grasping or yearning. The mountain just sits in its own completeness, lacking nothing.

When we sit like a mountain, we are not bothered by the comings and goings of thoughts, sensations, and emotions. We are steady, upright, without leaning toward this or away from that. We feel the strength and steadfastness of the mountain within every molecule; no part of us is left out. When we sit like a mountain, we feel deeply connected to the earth below and the sky above. We feel supported and protected, trusting that the suturing happens on its own. One breath, one stitch. One stitch, one breath.

Water Meditation: Lying Down. Lie down on your back in a comfortable position. As in the mountain meditation, begin with a calming and centering meditation, such as the one suggested in chapter one. Remind yourself your body is more than 90 percent liquid. So already, even before you begin the water meditation, you are flowing.

When you are ready, gently pay attention to the natural flow of your breath, letting it flow in and out without trying to control it or to make it smoother or deeper. Gently pay attention to your thoughts and emotions, letting them flow in and out.

Notice the contours of your body, and how sensations are always arising and dissolving. Experience the natural flow of life without clinging to anything, without avoiding anything. To cling, we first have to separate ourselves from the object of our clinging. To avoid, we first have to separate ourselves from the object we are avoiding.

Lying comfortably, feeling supported, allow yourself to trust your meditation. Trust that as you practice regularly, the impulse to cling or avoid gradually loosens up. It arises and dissolves as naturally as the flow of your own breath. Impulses, sensations, emotions, thoughts—all are part of the natural flow of life. No matter how strong or overpowering they feel, as long as they are flowing, you are being sutured. It happens on its own.

TWO EXERCISES FOR ADVANCED MEDITATION PRACTITIONERS

1. In meditation, try to experience the turbulence of thought and sensation as waves that you can surf. At times, you may experience a big wave of emotion. Other times repetitive thought waves seem to tumble over each other. You may soar to great heights on a cresting wave, or maybe you're deep inside the curl, surrounded by great emotional energy. Breathe. Whatever form they take, they are just waves. With practice, you may come to enjoy being in this wonderful ocean that includes all life.

2. In your meditation practice, notice that incessant mental chattering is often held together by the stickiness of a particular negative emotion: it may be anger, sadness, jealousy, despair, or something else. Scan your body for the specific sensations related to the emotion. Can you identify any areas of tightness, prickliness, or heat? Do these areas seem to increase in intensity

as you move your awareness into them? Can you stay with the sensation as it peaks? What happens? You may be surprised as the energy of the emotion begins to dissipate in response to your non-judgmental awareness. You may also notice that the incessant chattering has abated.

EIGHT

Brain Plasticity, Mirror Mind, and Enlightenment

As above, so below; as within, so without; as the universe, so the soul.

—HERMES TRISMEGISTUS

THE UNIVERSE IS NOT A THING. It is an ever-changing process, creating and re-creating itself moment by moment. It unfolds in specific forms and patterns, but within those forms and patterns, everything is always changing.

What is true for the universe is also true for our planet. All that arises does so within a process of becoming something else. From the moment winter arrives, it is moving toward spring. Ocean waves rise and subside, along with clouds, migrating birds, our breath, glaciers, mountains, and valleys.

The Heart Sutra, which is chanted every morning in most Zen centers around the world, says, "Form is emptiness; emptiness is form." This is just another way of saying that nothing is static. Within seven years, every cell in our body has been replaced, some many times over. The impermanent nature of all that exists is one of Buddha's most fundamental teachings. It says that all things are constantly coming and going. It sounds so simple. But experiencing our own malleability is not as simple as it sounds.

In private, one-to-one meetings with me, people often complain, "I'm feeling out of sorts. I haven't been feeling like myself lately." Maybe you've even felt this way. But who's the *you* that you're not feeling like? Is it the you who is stuck in the past, in some patterned behavior, or in a trance of unworthiness? Which you is more authentic, the you you're not feeling like, or the "out of sorts" you that you don't yet know?

When the self feels like an object rather than a process, we become rigid, always following the same routine, always the same thoughts running through our brain. So maybe we should not be so resistant to feeling out of sorts. Maybe we should even welcome it.

You begin by recognizing your reaction to feeling out of sorts. Do you get discouraged, bummed out, or depressed? Then you may try saying to yourself, "Oh, I am bumping into the wall that I've built around my idea of who I am." Here is your opportunity to explore the contours and textures of a wall that is usually invisible to you. You may recognize that you've always felt trapped inside this idea of who you are.

In meditation, your gentle awareness penetrates the wall. Eventually, what felt like a wall becomes more like a boundary. A boundary is penetrable. It is crossable. Maybe you feel out of sorts because boundaries are places where change happens very quickly. Boundaries are inherently unstable and unpredictable—the boundaries between countries, shorelines, front lines, weather fronts, the boundary between you and not-you, between past and present, between present and future. Boundaries are places of mystery, of the unknown.

The next time you feel out of sorts, rather than withdrawing and creating a wall, move very close to the feeling, so close you merge with it. You may discover what Buddha discovered twenty-five hundred years ago, what modern science is now validating: the barrier is the gate.

BRAIN PLASTICITY: THE BARRIER IS THE GATE

> Once through the gate, the discovery is made that the
>   gate is
> not actually a barrier or an opening through which to
>   pass.
> It is simply reality presenting itself.
>
> —MAEZUMI ROSHI

Once a monk requested a meeting with his teacher to complain about how badly things were going for him in the monastery. After hearing the monk's litany of complaints, the master said, "Why don't you leave?"

Disheartened, the monk started for the door.

"Not that door," the teacher said.

The monk turned and started for another door.

"Not that door," the teacher said.

Exasperated, the monk started for the last door, but again the teacher said, "Not that door."

"But there are no other doors!"

"Yes, there are no doors," the teacher replied calmly. "So I guess you will have to stay."

At that moment, the monk's exasperation dropped away. His desire for things to be other than what they were dissolved. The doors, gates, and barriers in his mind vanished, and he experienced great spaciousness and deep quiet.

This is a typical Zen story. It points out that what we experience as barriers are self-created and sustained by nothing more substantial than a thought that is repeated over and over.

I'm a big believer in meditation retreats. For extended periods—two days, five days, seven days—we block out the chattering mind so we can experience something beyond our usual small egoic self. At retreats, there is nowhere to go and nothing to do. Our focus is turned inward, and outer distractions are minimized. We don't talk, we don't make eye contact or communicate in any way. We don't read, text, or e-mail; we sustain a heightened state of awareness. Our focus is inward.

Early in the retreat, we usually experience our fears, desires, and aversions as barriers to a still mind. Eventually, we realize that it is actually our conditioned reactivity to fear, desire, and aversion that keeps us stirred up. With meditative awareness, we look closely at what we perceive as barriers and hindrances until we can see through them. Then we realize that the barrier was actually a gateway to clear-seeing. When we see beyond a barrier, our brain changes; new neural pathways are created. The more neural pathways we have, the more freedom we experience.

Historically, the brain was thought of as a machine with distinct, local parts—an auditory center, a visual center, a specific area responsible for our sense of smell, another for our sense of pain or pleasure. Each of these centers was believed to be discrete and localized—walled up. Common sense told us that we see with our eyes, hear with our ears, taste with our tongues, smell with our noses, and feel with our skin. So if one of these centers breaks down—the visual center, for example—there is no solution. The person is permanently blind.

But, as I mentioned earlier, Buddha taught that nothing was permanent. Now scientists are confirming this truth. Until the 1980s, brain scientists were convinced that there was no plasticity in the adult brain. Today we know that age alone has little, if any, negative effect on our brain. Our brain becomes more and more complex throughout our lifetime, and even can reorganize itself in response to injury. The brain's capacity to create new pathways is known as *neural plasticity*.

In his book *The Brain That Changes Itself*, psychiatrist Norman Doidge writes, "If the brain can reorganize itself, simple local-izationism cannot be a correct image of the brain." The simplest way to think about brain plasticity is that it means "openness." There are no walls that divide up the brain's functioning. If each section were walled off, the brain would be unable to reorganize and make the kinds of adjustments that have been seen and doc-umented by modern science.

SYNESTHESIA: SEEING SOUNDS AND HEARING COLORS

Like the fingers on your hand, like an hourglass of sand,
We can separate but not divide.

—LEONARD COHEN, "DEMOCRACY"

In earlier chapters, we looked closely at our deeply ingrained ideas about what it's like to be a human being, about our self-worth and the worthiness of all things, and about sex, money, failure, humility, and the world itself. But now we're approaching some-thing much more challenging. Deconstructing our ideas is one thing; deconstructing our immediate sensory experience—our sense of sight, sound, taste, smell, and touch—is quite another.

The neurologist Paul Bach-y-Rita (1934–2006) was one of the most recognized researchers in this new field of study. He discovered that skin and its touch receptors could actually be a substitute for the retina. Dr. Bach-y-Rita developed a device that enabled blind people to see. It involved a sort of tactile machine that was attached to their back and abdomen. With these devices, blind people could be trained to recognize shapes and track motion. Some could perceive the motion of a ball rolling across the floor. When taken to an electronics plant, some could even carry out assembly-line tasks.

Dr. Bach-y-Rita's discovery opened up a new field of scientific research. In follow-up studies, scientists have learned that our tongue may be the second-best place on the body for receiving and sending visual information to the brain. When a camera transferred images to the tongue, over time, participants began to perceive the stimulation as shapes and features in space. In other words, their tongue became a surrogate eye.

Images can also be converted to soundscapes and picked up by a blind person's ears. Participants in a study were blindfolded in such a way that no light at all was allowed in. After just one week, they were able to distinguish barriers in their path by the auditory echoes. Their ears become surrogate eyes.

The Heart Sutra, which says that form is completely empty, was written over two thousand years ago. It says, "No eyes, no ears, no nose, no tongue . . . no sight, no sound, no smell, no taste . . ." The sutra is not suggesting that eyes and sight do not exist. Rather, it is pointing out that our ability to see is not dependent on a single, isolated sense organ that we call "eyes."

What the Heart Sutra points out and what modern science has discovered is that, when we block out our most commonly used pathways, the polysensory nature of the brain is revealed. Likewise, when we block out our small, localized, egoic self, we experience something beyond it. We discover that it is only the constant chattering of our mind that makes us feel isolated and alone.

Creating boundaries where none actually exist does not alter reality, but it does limit our perception of reality—which means it limits our everyday experience. We see only with our eyes, when reality offers us the opportunity to "see" the world around us through a multiplicity of modes. How much fuller would our experience be if we not only *saw* shapes and colors, but felt them, tasted them, and heard their voices?

THE PLASTICITY PARADOX

Even though the brain is fluid and plastic, through brain noise, habit, and addiction the soft Play-Doh texture of the brain hardens.

—NORMAN DOIDGE

We now know that the brain is completely open and without fixed boundaries. Even so, our incessant mental chatter, habituated thought patterns, and other addictive behaviors create an unnatural rigidity within the Play-Doh texture of the brain. It is not age, but repetitive thoughts and behaviors that inhibit our brain's ability to grow new neural pathways throughout our lifetime.

Plasticity gives rise to flexibility. Yet paradoxically, plasticity can also lead to rigidity. If new behaviors become locked in through repetition, the brain's natural reward system can become a hindrance to the brain's natural plasticity.

The organic chemical dopamine, which is part of the neural reward system, is a primary cause of the brain's deterioration over time. Dopamine acts as a mediator between neurons. When it's released by the brain and kidneys, where it is synthesized, we experience a surge of pleasure and confidence—strong motivation to repeat whatever we did to initiate the release. When dopamine is released in excess, it becomes an intoxicant, locking us into addictive behaviors and hindering the brain's natural ability to respond in fresh new ways.

Our primary addiction is to the chattering mind, which sustains and reinforces the belief in a separate self. But mental chatter doesn't activate a dopamine release. Because we're in pain from that addiction, we turn to secondary addictions for the dopamine.

In the twenty-first century, our two biggest secondary addictions are computer related—computer porn and electronic games. We see these addictions all the time, in adults and children. In *Nothing Holy about It*, I told the story of a friend who became addicted to porn after a painful divorce. Next time you are in a restaurant, look around and see how many children are too busy playing electronic games to eat. Recently, we took our grandsons to Disney World in Florida. We actually had to makes rules to restrict their internet time even though we were surrounded by all kinds of amusements.

In Buddhism, we have a precept that states, "I will refrain from indulging in intoxicants." Intoxicants include activities that abuse the brain's natural reward system. If we honor this precept, the brain retains its plasticity. Unfortunately, once plasticity is lost, it takes a lot to restore the soft Play-Doh texture. Even then, the brain's ability to regulate itself may be more fragile after it has been compromised.

A natural aspect of freedom is openness. When we're carrying around a lot of habituated behaviors, there is no room for openness. We feel walled in.

Many neurologists now recommend two activities to maintain brain plasticity: novelty and meditation.

Novelty means learning new skills like dancing, riding a bike, or a new language—anything that you haven't done before. My son-in-law, Eric, is from France. When he and my daughter, Erin, got married, they had a big wedding in France. At the reception, my wife, Linda, and I were expected to dance the first dance, along with Erin and Eric, and Eric's parents. This was a very formal wedding, and the first dance was to be a waltz. I hadn't danced in years—and even when I did dance, it wasn't ballroom dancing.

So Linda and I took lessons. Once a week for several weeks, and between lessons we practiced at home. Of course, Linda caught on right away. She always seems to learn new things easily. I was a klutz. My dancing was awful. But I didn't want to let my daughter down or embarrass myself in front of hundreds of people, so I stayed with it. Life is always offering opportunities for us to create new neural pathways. All we have to do is say yes more often.

But learning new skills involves frustration. Learning to waltz involved *a lot* of frustration. Here is where the second recommendation by neuroscientists comes in: meditation. When we meditate, frustration and discouragement are common companions. We learn to recognize them as they are arising. We get to know them intimately, so we're not blindsided and overwhelmed by them. They become like distant cousins whom we don't particularly enjoy but whom we treat kindly when they visit.

Learning new skills also requires focus. On the island in the Caribbean where my family spends Christmas, there are a lot of monkeys and a lot of fruit trees. The monkeys leap from branch to branch, tree to tree, taking one or two bites from a fruit, and then tossing it to the ground. All day long, they do this.

Are human beings so different? In meditation, the first thing we notice is how easily we leap from one thought to another. People are always surprised to learn how difficult it is to stay focused on the breath. Beginners become distracted within seconds. In Buddhism, it is called "monkey mind." Easy to see why, right? Monkey mind is distracted mind.

Monkey mind is the leading cause of symptoms related to aging, like the diminished ability to find words, diminished short-term memory, and the inability to sustain a focused attention. But we now know that it is not age but the atrophy of our attentional system that is responsible for many of these symptoms. The capacity to focus and sustain our attention is like any other ability: if we don't use it, we lose it.

As our capacity to focus deteriorates, we rely more and more on habituated behaviors—a reliance that increases brain rigidity and decreases plasticity. Do you see the vicious cycle that we get trapped in? Meditative awareness allows us to see our patterns as they are forming before they become deeply ingrained. The key to freeing ourselves from habituated behaviors is seeing *in the moment* what is actually driving us, so we can intervene with a midcourse correction.

| KEY #8: Seeing is the beginning of freeing.

FROM MONKEY MIND TO MIRROR MIND

China's only female emperor, Empress Wu, lived in the eighth century. It's a remarkable story: She went from concubine to emperor and ruled China for twenty years. Some say they were among the most peaceful, influential, and productive years in China's history. Empress Wu was also an ardent supporter of Buddhism.

Once, so the story goes, Empress Wu asked the court councilor, Zen master Fazang, to explain the relationship between the one and the many. To demonstrate, Fazang strung large mirrors along the walls and in the corners, ceiling, and floor of a chamber in the palace. In the center of the room, a single candle hung from the ceiling. When it was lit, an endless web of reflected light crisscrossed the chamber, creating an infinite series of images within images, each containing the flame.

"How lovely," Empress Wu exclaimed. "Within many, one."

Fazang then opened his palm and in it sat a small crystal ball, which simultaneously contained all the flames. Empress Wu clearly saw how the infinitely large could be contained within the small. She immediately understood how the pain and joy experienced by one is simultaneously transmitted to the many.

The Taoists, who deeply value the teachings of nature, have a similar metaphor. Imagine a still mountain lake surrounded by dense forest. The surface of the lake is like a mirror. It perfectly reflects the surrounding trees, the animals that approach its shore, and even the sun, moon, and stars. When a cloud passes over, it is reflected perfectly. Birds flying over are reflected perfectly—but once they have passed over no trace is left behind. In Taoism, clouds are a metaphor for delusion and birds a metaphor for thoughts. When we allow them to just pass over without clinging to them, our view of reality remains clear and undistorted.

Mental noise disturbs a still mind as the wind disturbs a still lake. When a strong wind whips up and churns its surface, clarity is lost. But down deep, the water remains still. From these depths, we can see beyond the foamy whitecaps. The clear blue sky is still there. It is always there.

Stillness and mirror-like clarity are innate qualities of our mind that are always available to us. It's only our constant mental chattering that keeps us feeling churned up and leaping from thought to thought. But monkey mind is not our natural mental state. And now modern science has found evidence that seems to support what Buddhism has been teaching for centuries.

ANCIENT WISDOM/MODERN SCIENCE: THE DISCOVERY OF MIRROR NEURONS

> I predict that mirror neurons will do for psychology what DNA did for biology.
>
> —V. S. RAMACHANDRAN

During the 1980s, researchers at the University of Parma in Italy were studying the part of the brain responsible for movement. In the study, monkeys were offered peanuts while hooked up to electrodes to monitor the activity of specific neurons. Each time the monkey picked up a peanut to eat, the monitor would go click, click, click to signal neural activity.

One day, a researcher began to snack on a handful of peanuts. Click, click, click. Surprised, the researcher looked from the monitor to the monkey. What he saw was totally unexpected: As the monkey *watched* the researcher eat the peanuts, the area in his brain responsible for hand and mouth movement was lit up—yet the monkey was completely still. What was going on?

Since then, this experiment has been repeated numerous times with the same result. In one study, a participant was touched by a feather while another watched. Both brains lit up as if both were feeling the touch of the feather. Another study revealed that participants do not even have to be in the same room. A group of participants were hooked up to monitors and scanned while listening to a recording of a story. The storyteller had recorded the story earlier, while he himself was being scanned. The brains of the storyteller and the listeners lit up in the same places at the same time in the story.

Scientists are calling the neurons responsible for this surprising phenomenon *mirror neurons*. In each of these studies, one common element was crucial to the success of the experiment: present moment awareness. The more attentive the witness, the greater the response.

Mirror neurons allow us to learn a desired activity or response through resonating with another person, such as a role model, mentor, or teacher. When we see our mentor walking a certain path, we are inclined to walk the same path ourselves because, through mirror neurons, we have already walked the path and it is familiar to us. Furthermore, since neurons multiply according to how often they're used, the more we rely on mentors and role models, the more mirror neurons we have.

As our brain learns to recognize and appreciate its own mirror-like capacity, we expand our mental perspectives beyond the limitations of a separate, isolated self. In meditation, as we learn to relax into these boundless experiences, our brain learns to trust its expansive capacities.

THE SCIENCE OF EMPATHY

It now seems clear that an isolated, separate self cannot be an appropriate or accurate self-image. A deep empathic connection with others is biological, beyond conscious control, and bridges space and time. When someone we love is in pain, we feel it too. When a stranger falls on the street, we cringe inside. As we watch a movie, our emotions run the gamut between despair and exhilaration along with the emotions of the characters we are watching. The feeling of pride when our country's top athlete takes the center ring and receives the gold metal—this, too, is the work of our mirror neurons.

Buddhist psychology understands consciousness as a unified field that has an aspect of localization. Imagine a drop of water falling toward the ocean. A raindrop holds its shape, its identity as rain, through surface tension. But as soon as it touches the ocean, the tension is released.

In meditation, we learn to let go of our fear-based ideas that keep us in a narrow-minded, contracted state. Just as brain plasticity is hindered by conditioned, habituated reactions, so too is our empathic connection to the world around us. To attune ourselves to the emotions of another, we have to let go of what we think we know and relax into Big Mind.

It is paradoxical, yet true, to say that the more we know, the more ignorant we become in the absolute sense, for it is only through enlightenment that we become conscious of our limitations.

—NIKOLA TESLA

DOING THE WORK

Please consider keeping a journal devoted to increasing your brain's plasticity. Here are a few questions and exercises to help you get started.

1. What are your intoxicants, the addictive behaviors that hinder your brain's natural ability to respond in fresh new ways? Choose a habit that is cemented into your daily routine, like drinking coffee or tea, or reading your e-mails early in the morning. Stop doing it for a week and allow yourself to experience the discomfort or disorientation you feel without it. Every time you feel uncomfortable, bring your attention back to your breath and/or other sensations in your body.

2. For a period of one week, notice the times you bump into the wall that you've built around your idea of who you are. What

are the contours and textures of that wall? What idea about who you are does it create? What idea about who you are traps you? What happens when you allow that wall to become permeable, to become a boundary? How does that wall become a gate?

3. For one week, notice the barriers you create, such as fears, desires, aversions, and your conditioned reactivity to these emotions. What thoughts do you repeat over and over to sustain them? Write them down. Keep a list.

4. When you recognize a commonly used pathway in your chattering mind, what happens if you choose to block that well-used route of the small, egoic self? What are you able to see, hear, taste? What happens to your isolated self?

5. Over the course of one week, watch for moments of discouragement, fear, or other negative emotions. What habituated behaviors kick in? What habitual thoughts does the chattering mind produce? How can you intervene in the moment and make a midcourse correction? Under the ruffled surface, what does your clear and undistorted view of reality look like?

6. Think about an activity that you have considered doing, but have resisted because it feels awkward. Commit to it for one month. Each time you feel like quitting because you are "no good at it," remind yourself that by sticking with it you are increasing your neural plasticity.

NINE

Transforming Knowledge into Wisdom through Everyday Life

Once upon a time, in a not-so-faraway land, there was a kingdom of acorns nestled in the shade of a grand oak tree. Since the citizens of this kingdom were modern and fully westernized acorns, they went about their business with purposeful energy; and since they were midlife, baby-boomer acorns, they engaged in a lot of self-reflection and self-help courses.

There were seminars called "Getting All You Can out of Your Shell." There were woundedness and recovery groups for those who had been bruised in their original fall from the tree. There were retreats and spas for oiling and polishing their shells, and various acornopathic therapies to enhance longevity and well-being.

One day, there suddenly appeared in the kingdom a knotty little stranger who'd apparently been dropped out of the blue by a passing bird. He was odd, capless, and dirty. Crouched beneath the oak tree, he began to stammer out a strange and wild tale. Pointing upward at the tree, he spoke to all that would listen to him, and said, "We . . . are . . . that!"

"Delusional thinking, obviously," the distinguished citizens around him concluded.

A few, however, were curious and amused. They continued to engage the stranger in conversation. "So tell us, how would we become that tree?"

"Well," said the stranger, pointing downward, "it has something to do with going into the ground—and cracking open the shell."

The citizens were aghast. "Insane," one replied.

"Totally morbid!" exclaimed another.

"Why, then," said a third, "we wouldn't be acorns anymore!"

BREAKING THROUGH THE EGO SHELL

As human beings, we believe that self-knowledge is important. Other creatures may love and laugh, talk and think—but we reflect, which brings depth and texture to what may otherwise be a pretty flat and shallow existence. We are also aware of the limits of our knowledge—and we're both fascinated and frustrated that our own existence is the most difficult thing for us to know and understand.

Self-reflection, if not managed skillfully, can lead to vicious cycles of confusion. We feel isolated and lonely when we're caught in our reflective mode, so we tend to create myths to make sense of our loneliness. We create gods and buddhas, heavens and hells, ideas about falling from grace or getting a second chance through reincarnation. The more we cling to our chosen myths, the more closed down and isolated we become. It is a self-sustaining cycle.

The story about the acorn and the oak tree suggests that our ego shell consists of our ideas about ourselves, our world, and our place in the grand scheme of things. A shell is a protective layer. For an acorn to realize the truth that it is an oak tree, the acorn must be willing to sink into the ground and break through the shell. It must let go of its strongly held idea of who and what it actually is.

Likewise, we human beings must be willing to sink down into the ground of our being and allow our ego shell to dissolve. But where did this shell come from in the first place? We create protective layers through the process of attachment. When we become attached to an idea, we are no longer free to explore. Our mind closes up around that idea, and our world becomes smaller and smaller, excluding everything that doesn't align with our narrow understanding of reality. This is what is meant by attachment.

Spiritual maturity requires nonattachment. This can be confusing for people. Once I was speaking to a small group of newcomers at the Minnesota Zen Meditation Center about spiritual maturity and the Buddhist concept of nonattachment. Afterward, someone came up to me and expressed her frustration. "I want to have a family," she said. "I want kids. What will happen to my relationships with nonattachment? How can I love with nonattachment?"

Her confusion is understandable. An English dictionary defines nonattachment as "indifference, separation, aloofness, isolation." From a psychological standpoint, attachment is an important aspect within our development. This is true for the development of all mammals. So psychologically, this definition of nonattachment is a serious developmental problem.

The Buddhist idea of nonattachment is very different from the dictionary definition. Nonattachment, from a Buddhist perspective, is always coupled with intimacy, which is closeness and non-separation. Maturity, whether we're talking about spiritual maturity or mature love between two people, involves going beyond attachment. As the acorn story suggests, the path to maturity begins when we become willing to let go of our protective shell. It happens naturally.

When my grandson was two years old, he became very attached to me. He smiled when I gave him what he wanted—candy or ice cream—and jumped into my arms as if he was the most lovable being in the world. He cried when I had to leave or when I didn't give him what he wanted. He was trying to control me.

My two-year-old grandson didn't yet know how to manipulate me in sophisticated ways, but his big brother, who was five at the time, had all sorts of subtle ways of using me to get his needs met, like asking me to tell him the same story over and over and correcting me along the way. It was important to him to feel accepted, secure, and empowered. At that stage of his development, those feelings came through his relationships with the adults in his life.

Although it was necessary for my grandsons to go through the attachment stage, it was also necessary for them to outgrow it so that I could be more to them than just a candy-giver. Non-attachment means that I can be myself and you'll accept me, and that you can be yourself and I'll accept you. This is real intimacy, without attachment. We're not trying to use each other to feel secure and empowered. Cultivating the capacity for true intimacy, which is never based on control or manipulation, is a major task of adulthood.

The acorn story is a well-known parable entitled "Acornology." It has been told and retold since the 1950s, when it was written by the British psychologist Maurice Nicoll. I came across it in Rev. Cynthia Bourgeault's wonderful book *The Wisdom Way of Knowing*. A much older parable that carries the same message is told in the Upanishads, a Hindu text that dates back to 800 B.C.E., which predates both Buddha and the early Taoists. It is the story of a father speaking to his son.

The father said, "The rivers in the east flow eastward, the rivers in the west flow westward, and all enter the seas. From sea to sea they pass, the clouds lifting them to the sky as vapor and sending them down as rain. And as the rivers, when they are united with the sea, do not know whether they are this river or that, likewise all creatures enter this world from the one essence—and, son, you are that."

Then, taking a fruit from a banyan tree, the father split it open and asked the son, "What do you see?"

"Seeds," the son replied.

The father split open the seeds and again asked, "What do you see?"

The son shook his head. He saw nothing clearly.

The father nodded. "You are unable to see the essence because within it is the whole of the banyan tree. That which is the subtle essence, in which all beings have their existence—my son, you are that."

LOOKING DEEPLY AT OUR CORE VALUES

The process of breaking through the ego shell begins by looking deeply at our core values. As Americans, we are fortunate. Our core values were outlined by our founding fathers in the Declaration of Independence and in the Constitution. These documents articulate the intrinsic value of the individual as well as the vital importance of interdependence.

The opening sentence of the Declaration of Independence points to the inalienable right of each individual to "life, liberty, and the pursuit of happiness." This core value corresponds directly to Buddha's teaching that everyone, regardless of race, gender, or status, has the potential to wake up to the timeless stillness at the core of all being, which is the basis for true happiness.

Our Constitution points to the importance of interdependence. It outlines a plan by which all the peoples of the United

States can work together to govern themselves and to create a unified, just, and mutually respectful society. This concept is reinforced through other cultural artifacts that all of us recognize. Years before we begin a meditation practice, in elementary school we learn to recite the words "one nation, indivisible, with liberty and justice for all" from the pledge of allegiance to the flag. (The phrase "under God" was added in 1954.) When we pledge our allegiance to one indivisible nation, we are also honoring all of its independent parts.

So the founding documents of the United States are more than just political. In a sense, they also reflect a core Zen Buddhist axiom: difference within oneness and oneness within difference, which is the nature of life itself. Unfortunately, this core value is not upheld for all people. Societies in the West and the East both fall short of this aspiration. But in the United States the aspiration is there, written into our Constitution from the very beginning.

Let's remember that the idea of individual rights and liberties was radical in 1776. European governments hadn't yet acknowledged an individual's independence and right to the pursuit of happiness. The movement toward both independence and interdependence was America's first counterculture. Was it really that much different from Jesus's counterculture two thousand years ago, or from Buddha's counterculture five hundred years before that?

If we look closely, we see elements of this counterculture popping up at sporadic moments throughout history. Four hundred years after Buddha, the Roman poet Virgil penned the words *e pluribus unum*, "out of many, one." He was referring to how each color of the rainbow was contained within a single color. The motto *"e pluribus unum"* became the foundation for our experiment in democracy nearly two thousand years later, appearing on the Great Seal of the United States and engraved on our currency.

We thrive individually and collectively only when we recognize and value our interdependence. This truth is self-evident from many different perspectives. Ecologically, we can see how our overdependence on fossil fuels is beginning to threaten the habitat and very existence of polar bears and other species that are on the verge of extinction. Economically, we see that when the New York stock exchange plunges, tremors are felt in cities and villages around the world. When America goes into a recession, the rest of the world follows.

I'm not suggesting that our founding fathers had actually experienced the oneness of all life and the deep stillness that Buddha's teachings point to. Nevertheless, the motto *e pluribus unum* can be a reminder and a beacon for meditators who are attempting to tap into their undivided heart.

To remember the next key concept, you won't need a sticky note on your refrigerator. You won't need to use it as a mantra for your meditation. You will be reminded of it every time you open your wallet.

> KEY #9: *E pluribus unum* is the key
> to an undivided heart.

It is impossible to heal ourselves without healing our world, because we are not separate from our world. Yet we introduce hundreds of potentially dangerous chemicals into our environment every day, changing our biochemistry and perhaps even beginning to degrade our genetic code. When it comes to the environment, we seem to be ignoring a core American value, as expressed by *e pluribus unum*. A creature that reveals a lot about the concept of a dualistic practice with a non-dualistic attitude is the sea sponge. A sponge exists by pumping water through its body. Water flows through its internal canals, bringing nutrients and removing toxins.

Sometimes the water is too warm or too cold, but the sponge just takes it in and receives the nutrients that are offered. If the sponge becomes rigid and calcified, water can no longer flow through its canals. The trapped water becomes polluted, and the sponge dies.

The sponge cannot live in isolation, and neither can we. In meditation, we learn how to keep the water flowing. Sometimes the current brings sadness and loss; sometimes it brings joy and prosperity. By staying open even when the water is too cold or too warm, we can experience a natural communion with all that exists.

The water inside the sponge is not separate from the melting Arctic ice sheet and Antarctic glaciers. It's not separate from the vaporized water in our atmosphere, some of which may have been carried to Earth by comets from other parts of the universe. It is the stuff of the universe flowing through a tiny, seemingly insignificant sponge. But how insignificant can the sponge be if it is nurtured and nourished by the entire universe?

A sponge stays alive by remaining open to its environment. This is what Suzuki Roshi called a dualistic practice: there is a sponge and there is an environment—two separate things that are deeply interconnected.

When I was studying with Suzuki back in the 1960s, Zen students often disparaged the dualistic view of the world, saying dismissively, "Oh that's just dualism." But Suzuki did not encourage this way of thinking. That's why he said, "We do a dualistic practice with a non-dualistic attitude."

Dualistic simply refers to seeing and experiencing the world through the lens of self and other, this and that, inside and outside. A non-dualistic attitude allows us to live in a dualistic world while remaining aware that everything we encounter and experience is the manifestation of one single process. Non-dualism is about keeping our pores open so life can flow through—as practiced by the sponge.

When we think, "I want to improve my life," or "I want to have a better relationship with others," we are engaging in a dualistic practice. To achieve these goals, I need to try to let go of my defensiveness, self-centeredness, and my territoriality so I can just be with you and connect with you in a genuine way.

It's easy to be open when the temperature of the water is just right, but when the water is too hot or too cold, we want to build barriers to keep it out. To stay open when the water feels too cold or too warm, we have to give up our primitive way of thinking. Fear and isolation make fundamentalists of us all. We become fundamentalist atheists, fundamentalist Christians, fundamentalist agnostics, fundamentalist Buddhists. Fundamentalism is the way of the calcified sponge. Don't be a calcified sponge; be a human being.

Focusing on our breath in meditation is a dualistic practice that helps us still and open our minds so we feel connected. Bringing our attention to our activity, over and over, is also a dualistic practice. Using a mantra is another dualistic practice. Even cultivating a deep aspiration to realize non-duality is a dualistic practice. We aspire to realize something that at first seems foreign to us. We aspire to not be dominated by the little guy in our head who is always pissing and moaning about things. We aspire to take care of our small self, but to also see beyond it to our fundamental non-dual nature. We aspire to know that this little wave is also the ocean. We aspire to practice *e pluribus unum*, which is a dualistic practice that is cultivated and sustained by a non-dualistic attitude.

Let's embrace it, okay?

In the 1970s, neurosurgeon Benjamin Libet was involved in research investigating human consciousness and free will. Dr. Libet made a dramatic discovery that suggests why meditation can be a powerful tool for bringing intelligence to our emotional lives.

Dr. Libet conducted a series of experiments with patients during brain surgery, when they were anesthetized but alert. (It was important that patients remain awake and alert throughout the procedure because communication between patient and surgeon was crucial.) As he monitored the electrical activity in the patient's brain, he asked the patient to move his finger. Using a clock that tracked time to the thousandths of a second, the patient was able to report the precise moment when they became aware of the urge to move the finger. This allowed Dr. Libet to see when the brain actually began activity that would culminate in the movement. In short, it let him separate the moment of awareness of the intent to move from the moment of actual action.

Dr. Libet discovered that the part of the brain that regulates movement lit up a quarter of a second before people became aware of their intent to move the finger. In other words, the brain acts on an impulse before we're even aware of our intention to act.

Fortunately, Dr. Libet's experiment didn't end there. Once we become aware of the intent to move, there is another quarter-second before the movement begins. This quarter-second window is crucial. It is the moment when we have the freedom to both discover and settle into the space that surrounds each impulse and decide whether to act on it.

So how do we access that quarter-second gap and remain in the driver's seat of our lives, especially when we are experiencing a strong emotion? The answer is simple: through our daily meditation practice. When we are persistent in practice, little by little we develop the ability to access these quarter-seconds, and we can begin to employ this ability in our daily lives.

In 1995, Daniel Goleman popularized the term *emotional intelligence*, which he defined as "the ability to monitor one's own and other peoples' emotions, to discriminate between different emotions and label them appropriately, to be empathic, and to use emotional information to guide thinking and behavior." In his book, *Emotional Intelligence*, Goleman talks about how strong emotions highjack our lives. Impulse is inherent in any strong emotion: anger translates into lashing out at others or at ourselves, fear becomes withdrawal and freezing up, hurt becomes tears.

Meditative awareness of the quarter-second gap allows us to free ourselves from the chain of reactivity and choose a different response. This means we are not owned by our conditioned thoughts, patterns, and impulses. Through our sitting practice, we become aware of thousands of quarter-seconds and learn to find deep composure and stillness as we access one after another—choosing each time whether to act on what has arisen. How lucky we are to be able to transform ourselves through this simple practice of bare awareness (or mindfulness).

Of course, this kind of freedom comes with a price. It takes time, effort, and patience to break out of our patterned behavior. We have to slow down our thoughts enough to see them. Otherwise, the quarter-second gap comes and goes so quickly we miss it. Slowing down our thoughts so we can see the gaps between them creates the possibility to intervene, to make a course correction. Developing this skill is often difficult and confusing, but we can no longer be content to live on autopilot, allowing ourselves to be driven continually by impulse and emotional reactivity and missing the wonderful freedom that surrounds all thought and emotion.

Habituated behaviors are convenient and often helpful, but with overuse even our strengths can become weaknesses; our patterns can become a crutch. When we are trapped in a pattern, we're stuck in the past. Nuance and freshness are lost. Subtlety and intimacy are lost. Meditation practice allows us to see the blind spots that habitual patterns create. By working with the quarter-second gap, we're able to meet life directly, moment by moment, with fresh eyes.

As we learn to settle into the wonderful stillness that manifests itself in one quarter-second after another, we can gradually free ourselves from addictive emotional responses and experience a sense of non-separation, which Buddhist philosophers call non-dualism. That's a big word for the simple, timeless freedom that is always available to us.

You may be wondering how you could possibly realize anything in a quarter-second. But you needn't worry about how quickly a quarter of a second passes. Within timelessness, a quarter of a second is much longer than you think!

DOING THE WORK

The following are four practices that help us to experience stillness and connectedness. Try writing up a commitment sheet and signing it. Commit to engaging in at least one of the following practices for fifteen minutes each day, and share it with one friend who agrees to hold you accountable.

1. *Sitting meditation.* Sitting in an upright posture is best. Even sitting outside is okay, so long as you don't get distracted.

2. *Meditation in action.* Bring your full attention to your activity, whether you're drinking a glass of water or listening to someone

who is suffering. If you start to get agitated or upset, you can bring your awareness to your breathing, anchoring yourself there so you don't get tossed away by your strong emotions. Or, for example, rather than swearing at someone for cutting you off on the freeway, repeat a mantra instead. No matter what is going on outside, practice continuously.

3. *Cultivating compassion.* Spend fifteen minutes reflecting on a difficult relationship. Whatever story you are telling yourself about it, create an opposite story. Allow this opposite story to impact you emotionally. Do not try to force yourself to believe it. For fifteen minutes, simply embrace it as a possibility. Compassion is not a passive emotion. We aspire to it. Maybe we fell short in the last moment, but we aspire to it in the next moment. You cultivate compassion by paying attention to your heart.

4. *Cultivating an abiding aspiration.* Do a fifteen-minute timed writing exercise to explore your personal aspiration for spiritual maturity. Like cultivating compassion, this is a dualistic practice because we aspire to realize something that we haven't realized. We aspire to stop seeing life as a tool that either sustains or endangers us. We aspire to manifest the stillness that is within each of us. We aspire to take care of our small self who is always pissing and moaning, and at the same time, we aspire to see beyond it to our wonderful interconnected nature.

Remember that dualistic practices are done with a non-dual orientation or sensibility. As we cultivate the capacity to sustain a non-dual consciousness, our attachment to a separate identity begins to dissolve. Compassion, spontaneity, and openness become our natural way of being in the world.

TEN

Living and Dying in a State of Readiness

IN MEDITATION, WE STEEP OURSELVES in a stillness that is beyond time. But people often get discouraged because too often it feels as if we're steeping in our constantly churning, constantly chattering mind—our worries, moods, regrets, and heartaches. When we begin meditating, and often for a long time, our thoughts come so fast they seem to trip over each other. If we do get a moment of quiet, it's fleeting and tentative; then we're back, immersed in the chatter of a busy mind, wondering if it's even worth our effort. We all feel this way from time to time.

But if we stick to our practice, we begin to see the underlying fear below our persistent mental noise. We begin to see how chatter, chatter, chatter covers up what we don't want to deal with. It is difficult to experience our deepest hurts, longings, and existential pain in a direct and undiluted way. With a sincere meditation practice, however, there is no avoiding these deepest feelings.

When we see our persistent thoughts without engaging or indulging them, this is pretty good. Eventually, the thoughts become transparent to us, and we begin to see the patterns from which they arise.

This often begins with an elusive and indistinct sense that something important is happening whose significance is just out of reach, like a vague shape just beyond the horizon of our awareness. It takes time for our inner eyes to adjust to the dark and to the sensation-based language of our inner teachers. We quickly get caught up in regretting the past and rehearsing for the future.

People often tell me they can't meditate because their thoughts are too loud, too busy, too out of control. They are convinced that their meditative experience is different from that of others. But everybody says that. So if everyone says it, what is really going on?

. . . if my thought-dreams could be seen
They'd probably put my head in a guillotine

—BOB DYLAN

Our "thought-dreams," or mental movies, spin around and around, binding us to the wheel of reacting, regretting, and rehearsing. The wheel becomes the driving force of our life, cutting us off from our true interconnected nature. It feels as if we are stuck in what Zen teacher Charlotte Joko Beck called "a substitute life."

When we step back from all our regretting and rehearsing just a little bit, we see that the world is much bigger and much warmer than we ever imagined. If we see the wheel of reactivity without judgment, there's a chance we can learn to disidentify with it. But we can't do it by *trying* to disidentify. If you're trying, then you're still caught on the wheel of should and shouldn't. You have just moved to a different spot.

Instead of getting distracted by the *content* of your thought-dreams, look instead at the *context* within which they arise. What is the emotional environment surrounding them? Is it fear? Frustration? Worry? This is when our churning mind becomes our teacher, revealing fixations and patterns, while turning us toward the moment-by-moment cultivation of mental clarity, courage, and inner strength.

But you have to steep yourself in the practice of sitting quietly and being aware, again and again and again, to get a sense of what I am talking about. You have to put the teabag in the hot water, over and over. Eventually, the flavor of the water changes; it becomes sweet, and that sweetness bubbles up right in the middle of your churning mind. Eventually you find that you aren't getting so wigged out over things.

There's no need for despair if you only get a fleeting taste of this stillness, because it is not of time—although it completely permeates time. The poet T. S. Eliot called it "the still point of the turning world." After a while, the still point begins to enter our consciousness when we least expect it. We taste it when we immerse ourselves in nature, when we feel a sense of intimacy with others or the world around us, or when we give ourselves fully to the simple activities of daily life. Regardless of the speed of your churning mind, the still point is there, waiting for you to tap into it.

As we learn to access this still point, we develop the ability to live each moment in a state of readiness, which includes a readiness to die. We move beyond the schism between life and death. Death is going on all around us, all the time. Gradually, we let go of our substitute life and face each moment directly—on life's terms, rather than our own. But how do we do that?

A Zen koan says:

Medicine and sickness heal each other.
All the world is medicine.

Seeing medicine and sickness as opposite sides of the same coin is a non-dualistic approach to healing. The fact that medicine can both heal and kill is the basis for homeopathic medicine and for vaccines. A vaccine introduces our immune system to a small amount of a specific type of disease so it can learn how to deal with it.

Meditation works the same way. We experience agitation when we sit still and try to focus on our breath, constantly having to bring our awareness back, again and again. Moment by moment, we bring our gentle awareness to the bodily sensations associated with agitation. We don't try to avoid or deny the unpleasant sensations and emotions that arise. Over time, we learn to deal with agitation caused by distraction and mental noise. Then, when a big agitation or a strong emotion comes along, our body knows how to deal with it without becoming overwhelmed. We have been immunized through familiarity.

Meditative awareness allows us to see deeply into the circumstances of our life. We learn something about ourselves. As we become more and more familiar with our responses, we learn to recognize those that empower us and those that imprison us, trapping us in repetitive patterns. We learn how to experience frustration, agitation, and emotional disturbances without being controlled or overcome by them. Empowerment is not about freedom *from* the chaotic energies of everyday life; it is freedom *within* those energies.

Medicine may also induce sickness. When I was young, I was allergic to poison oak. I used a homeopathic remedy, which means on a regular basis I took a small amount of the poison that I was allergic to. But once, I was distracted and took too much. My entire body swelled up.

Even experiences where the sense of a separate self drops away can be a source of illness. On the one hand, we feel a deep and joyful interconnectedness with all life. On the other hand, letting go of your separate identity can be extremely disorienting. These experiences are a natural outcome of meditation, but they may also arise suddenly through other circumstances, like illness, trauma, or drug use.

Setting is important. If the setting isn't supportive, an experience of boundlessness may induce paranoid delusions to shore up the lost boundaries, or grandiose thoughts that may include feelings of omniscience. A worst-case scenario may involve a psychotic episode. Mythologist Joseph Campbell said that the psychotic drowns in the same water that a mystic swims in. This is a case where medicine—an enlightenment experience—does, indeed, create illness.

Generally, however, meditation is the means through which all our experiences become medicine—that is, health-inducing. Meditation is a vaccine that gradually exposes us to boundlessness in a non-traumatic, non-chemical situation. It provides a structure for going beyond structure. However they are brought about, experiences of boundlessness allow the spirit to soar, whereas ordinary experiences keep us grounded.

There's a famous Zen story about a monk who, after an enlightenment experience, went to his teacher.

"The black ball soars through the starless night!" he exclaimed.

The teacher said, "That's very good, but continue your Zen practice for another year, and then come see me again."

A year later the student returned to his teacher. When asked to demonstrate his understanding of the way, he calmly replied, "I have breakfast at breakfast time and lunch at lunchtime."

LIVING AND DYING HEAL EACH OTHER

It's obvious that life without death is inconceivable. Fear of death, however, is a source of both psychological and physical suffering. This is a dilemma for us human beings. Resolving the great matter of life and death is what Zen practice is about.

Most of the world's religions are preoccupied with what happens after death. When my Roman Catholic grandmother was dying, she told me that she was hoping for purgatory because she felt that heaven was out of the question. My grandmother was one of the most caring and compassionate people I knew, but she judged herself very harshly. I thought, boy, that is a strict religion.

Today, however, most people are more preoccupied with denying death. We avoid thoughts about death and dying. The focus now is on keeping everyone alive through technology for as long as possible, even when they have minimal ability to function.

To cling to life and avoid death is fundamentally unnatural. Of course, we feel sad or grieve when we lose a loved one, or when we find our own health and youth fading. But if we can let this sadness enter our hearts completely, we have an opportunity to develop a deep acceptance of the natural ebb and flow of life. Denying the way of things keeps us on the wheel of reacting, regretting, and rehearsing. The wheel spins so fast we don't have time to love or grieve.

On the deepest level, "medicine and sickness heal each other" means that life and death heal each other. It points directly to the non-dual relationship between life and death. It says that life is death and death is life. A breath includes an inhale and an exhale; one provides the means for the other. In meditation, an appreciation of this reality begins to permeate our being, to penetrate down to our bones and marrow, inoculating us against our greatest fear.

MEETING DEATH IN A DEATH-PHOBIC CULTURE

You have to look very, very closely to see the interpenetration of life and death. To experience the intimate relationship between life and death, your mind has to be very still. But evidence of this relationship is all around us. Nature teaches us that life is not *here* and death *there*. It's life/death, death/life, life/death. From the moment we are born, we are both living and dying—at the same time.

Eva Saulitis was a writer and marine biologist who lived in Homer, Alaska, and studied whales in Prince William Sound. In her forties, she survived a bout with breast cancer. Ten years later, the cancer returned. This time, it had metastasized and the prognosis was different. She wrote about her experience in an exquisitely beautiful essay titled "Wild Darkness":

> For twenty-six Septembers I've hiked up streams littered with corpses of dying humpbacked salmon. It is nothing new, nothing surprising, not the stench, not the gore, not the thrashing of black humpies plowing past their dead brethren to spawn and die. It is familiar; still, it is terrible and wild. Winged and furred predators gather at the mouths of streams to pounce, pluck, tear, rip, and plunder the living, dying hordes. This September, it is just as terrible and wild as ever, but I gather in the scene with different eyes, the eyes of someone whose own demise is no longer an abstraction, the eyes of someone who has experienced the tears, rips, and plunder of cancer treatment.

Zen teaches that birth and death are not relegated to the past and the future because past and future are constructs of consciousness, not an innate quality of reality as it actually is. Sensations, emotions, and thoughts arise from darkness, unfold, and then dissolve back into darkness. This is the process that we call life.

Time is a form of measurement that we overlay onto the process. It is like a yardstick that measures change rather than distance. A yardstick translates space into units of measurement that we call distance, but neither the yardstick nor the units of measurement are innate qualities of space. Many of Zen's koans point to the mystery of life unfolding as time. Zen master Dogen referred to human beings as time-beings.

Reading Eva Saulitis's essay may evoke a felt-sense of this same mystery and paradox. One can almost feel the vivid, pulsing sensations of life/death, death/life arising together, unbidden and spontaneous, each bringing life to the other, each bringing death to the other. I'm not talking about life *after* death. Any ideas we have about what comes after we die are just ideas.

Experiencing the timeless, interpenetrating nature of life/death, death/life is the deepest level of existence we can experience as human beings. Might this be what Jesus meant when he said, "Before Abraham was, I am"? It certainly seems as if he is pointing to the mystery and paradox of life unfolding both within and beyond time.

As Saulitis struggled to meet her own impending death, her stepdaughter, named Eve, became pregnant. Watching Eve's body change throughout the pregnancy inspired Saulitis and gave her hope—not hope that her own body would somehow begin to pulse with new life, but hope that in the end her body would know what to do, would know how to meet the final moment.

Watching her body change . . . without aid of technology or study or experience, watching her simply embody pregnancy, should teach me something about dying. In preparation for giving birth, she reads how-to books, takes prenatal yoga, attends birthing classes. She studies and imagines. Yet no matter how learned she becomes, how well-informed, with the first contraction, her body will take over. It will enact the ancient, inborn process common to bears, goats, humans, whales, and field mice. She will inhabit her animal self. She will emit animal cries. She will experience the birth of her child; she will live it. Her body—not her will or her mind or even her self—will give birth.

From a Western point of view, death is the opposite of life. But death does not oppose life any more than the ocean opposes the waves that move across its surface. Life is not possible without death, in the same way that a wave is not possible without the ocean. Death is the very ground on which life exists.

In the United States, we tend to talk about ways to beat death, to escape it, rather than how to meet it. When it comes to meeting death, we are almost mute. Here is what Saulitis wrote about facing death in our death-denying culture:

Facing death in a death-phobic culture is lonely. But in wild places like Prince William Sound or the woods and sloughs behind my house, it is different. The salmon dying in their stream tell me I am not alone. The evidence is everywhere: in the skull of an immature eagle I found in the woods; in the bones of a moose in the gully below my house; in the corpse of a wasp on the windowsill; in the fall of a birch leaf from its branch. These things tell me death is true, right, graceful; not tragic, not failure, not defeat.

I would add that death is also life. Death is about giving ourselves away. The more we give ourselves to whatever is happening, to whatever we're doing, the more alive we feel in that very moment. Rather than being something that happens in the future, death is here, right now, and it is thoroughly permeated with life. The more fully we give ourselves away, the more freely life flows through us.

In the West, even when our body is ready to die, our culture doesn't allow it. People are told they must not die; they must fight it. Even when there is no quality of life left for them, even when there is no meaning, no aliveness or vitality in body or mind, people are told they must not give in to death. Our so-called health care system is about keeping people alive through technology for as long as possible, even with minimum functioning.

Learning how to die teaches us how to live. To reject the life/death nature of existence is to miss the fullness of life and exist in a state of fearfulness. It is not death, but fear, that robs us of life. If we let it, it will rob us to the very end.

HOPE AND FEAR CANNOT ALTER THE SEASON

Once, a farmer who had lost his wife asked a Buddhist priest to recite the Lotus Sutra to support her in the afterlife. After the recitation was over, the farmer asked, "Do you think my wife will benefit from this?"

"Not only your wife but all sentient beings benefit from the recitation of sutras," answered the priest.

"If all sentient beings benefit, my wife may be very weak and others may take advantage of her. So please recite the sutra just for her."

The priest explained that it was the desire of Buddhists to offer blessings and merit for every living being.

"That's a fine teaching," the farmer said, "but please make one exception. I have a neighbor who is rough and mean to me and even rougher and meaner to my wife. Just exclude him from all those sentient beings."

That's the human situation, isn't it? Too often, even at the time of death, ego-consciousness needs to build walls. Ego-consciousness is composed of hope and fear. Hope is about the future; fear comes from the past. Hoping and fearing are such deeply ingrained patterns we're blind to their negative effect on us.

In Western culture, we hold hope in the highest regard, as if wishing and hoping were our most important commodities. In reality, hope and fear are two sides of the same coin. Hope always involves fear. When we hope for a certain outcome, we fear that it may not come to pass. It is not hope that sustains us during difficult times; it is the courage to be simply and totally where we are.

Shakespeare wrote, "Cowards die many times before their deaths; the valiant never taste of death but once." We all understand what Shakespeare meant by that, and it does hold a piece of the truth. But an even deeper truth may be, "The valiant die a thousand deaths, but the coward neither lives nor dies."

The courageous person knows that living fully requires the willingness to die to each moment, giving oneself completely to every exhale, and then allowing the inhale to happen on its own. Each moment becomes like a torch burning at both ends, releasing tremendous energy. Then, when the last inhale comes, it's not such a big deal, because we know how to exhale completely. We know how to meet death because we've learned how to meet life. There is no attachment to the barrier we create between life and death, no walls to uphold, and nothing to defend or oppose.

Tibetan Buddhist teacher Trungpa Rinpoche said, "Hope and fear cannot alter the seasons." That means that hope and fear are not actually that important. So maybe we shouldn't invest so much energy in our hope and fear.

Disidentifying with our hope and fear is caring without being overly attached to the outcome. We have a choice. We can let uncertain times make us rigidly fearful, clinging to hope that things will be different, or we can let them become the basis for being more open, more kind, and more available for what scares us.

Instead of investing so much energy into hope and fear, maybe we should aspire to cultivate equanimity—in Buddhist terms, the balance that arises from clarity and wisdom. Equanimity is not born of hope or fear, or from indifference and apathy. It is born of clear-seeing. Practicing equanimity means that we don't invest so much time worrying about the future. Instead, we work from right here, in the only moment that matters, even when that moment is our last one.

Can there just be a leaving of our body when the time is ripe to leave it? You may ask, "How do I know if the time is ripe? What if I freeze and freak out?"

I sometimes say to my students that the ultimate test of a meditator's life is how he or she dies. The moment I say this, I often think, "I could freak out, myself!"

But so what? I don't have to worry about that. I can just enjoy being present now, knowing that, in Saulitis's beautiful words, "when death itself approaches I will enact the ancient, inborn process common to bears, goats, humans, whales, and field mice."

THE DEEPEST SELF-ACCEPTANCE

Buddha said, "Be a refuge unto yourself." He was including your *whole being*. Nothing is left out. Our humanity includes our feelings of unworthiness, and our concerns about sex, money, and getting our needs met. Being human includes falling down when we fail and then getting up. Falling down, we discover the wisdom of humility. Getting up, we experience spiritual liberation, what Dogen called riding the clouds and following the wind.

Embrace our whole being, and the entire world becomes medicine, offering exactly what we need, exactly when we need it. With a regular meditation practice, our consciousness expands wider and wider and wider, suturing all that was rent asunder. Eventually, we experience for ourselves what Buddha called our ultimate refuge.

Once there lived a boy made of salt who wanted to know where he came from. So he set out on a long journey that led him across snowcapped mountains and windblown plains. Along the way, he questioned everyone he met, asking where he came from. But no one could answer his burning question. Finally he arrived at the shore of the great ocean. The sea roared toward him, foaming and bubbling, and then halted and rushed away, beckoning to him.

"How marvelous," the boy exclaimed.

The tide seemed to whisper his name in a wordless way. It was a voiceless voice that was both strange and familiar. First, he dipped in his toe; and then he stepped tentatively into the foamy surf.

The ocean called to him, "If you wish to know who you are, you mustn't be afraid."

Hesitantly, the salt boy braved another step. "Ohhh!" he cried. Never had he experienced such joy! Exhilarated, he took another, then another, until he was running and splashing, going deeper and deeper—dissolving with each step—until there were no more questions, no more mountains to climb or plains to cross, no more worries or concerns.

"Ahhhh. Finally, I know who I am."

1. Please consider the story about the salt boy. Is it a story about dying or is it a story about living? In what way is it a story about both?

2. I've offered nine keys that can be called up immediately to help you to meet the challenges we all face. It seems appropriate, now, in this final chapter, to turn the tables by asking you to create your own key, one that speaks specifically to your own heart, to your undivided heart. When you're satisfied with your key, please e-mail it to me at tim@mnzencenter.org to share with others on our website. I would love to accompany you on your salt-boy journey.

Healing Our World, Together

Walnuts have a shell and they have a kernel.
Religions are the same.
They have an essence and they have a protective
coating.

—HUSTON SMITH

R ENOWNED AUTHOR AND TEACHER Huston Smith was born to a Christian missionary couple in a small village in China in 1919. In his youth, he aspired to follow in his parents' footsteps and become a missionary. But his life unfolded in a very unlikely and unusual way. He was a man driven by curiosity, inquiry, and enthusiasm for the spiritual life. What he called "internal revolutions" compelled him down many spiritual paths. Without abandoning his Christian roots, he practiced naturalistic theism, Buddhism, Hinduism, Taoism, and Islam.

Smith gave himself completely to the spiritual life—not in a zealous, fanatical way, but gently, skillfully. He was able to penetrate the protective shell of each tradition and sink deeply into their essence. For most of us, however, the shell seems impenetrable. We get caught by it, and end up judging and hurting each other.

While every religion has a protective shell, it seems most hard and dense in cases where there is one god who is the only real god and must be honored or prayed to in a specific manner. Even so, within all the major religions, there exists a contemplative (often referred to as *mystical* or *gnostic*) tradition where practitioners are able to penetrate the shell and tap into the essence of spiritual life.

Saint John of the Cross, for example, was summoned by the renowned mystic Saint Teresa of Avila to reform the Carmelite Order of Christian monks, of which he was a member. In his poem "The Dark Night of the Soul," he talks about abandoning the self and merging with God. German mystic Meister Eckhart echoes a similar experience. He said, "The eye with which I see God is the same eye with which God sees me. My eye and God's eye are one eye, one seeing, one knowing, one love."

Today, there are many Christian contemplatives who focus on the kind of seeing, knowing, and awakening that Meister Eckhart described. The practice of centering prayer, developed by Father Thomas Keating in the 1970s, is a nonpetitionary, meditative prayer that seems very similar to Zen meditation. If you're interested in Christian contemplative prayer, I highly recommend Rev. Cynthia Bourgeault's books, including *Centering Prayer and Inner Awakening* and *The Heart of Centering Prayer: Nondual Christianity in Theory and Practice*.

Kabbalah is the mystical side of Judaism. The essence of Kabbalah is that God cannot be comprehended by the human mind but can be experienced through the self-emptying of meditation. Hasidism, sometimes referred to as "Kabbalah for the people" because of its folksy stories and parables, also avoids the type of aggressive protectionism and promotion that the protective shell often stirs up.

The contemplative side of Islam is Sufism. And, of course, the best-known Sufi mystic is Rumi, the thirteenth-century Turkish poet whose works are widely known and loved in the West. Rumi's poem "Only Breath" was translated by Coleman Barks in his book *The Essential Rumi*:

> Not Christian or Jew or Muslim, not Hindu
> Buddhist, Sufi, or Zen. Not any religion
> or cultural system. I am not from the East
> or the West, not out of the ocean or up
> from the ground, not natural or ethereal, not
> composed of elements at all. I do not exist,
> am not an entity in this world or in the next,
> did not descend from Adam and Eve or any
> origin story. My place is placeless, a trace
> of the traceless. Neither body or soul.
> I belong to the beloved, have seen the two
> worlds as one and that one call to and know,
> first, last, outer, inner, only that
> breath breathing human being.

Too often, we focus on the difference between Eastern and Western religions. But are they really so different? Where Western religions speak of "sin," Eastern religions speak of "ignorance." Where Western contemplatives talk about realizing a oneness with God, Eastern sages talk about realizing an interconnectedness with all life.

Meister Eckhart wrote, "In the godhead there is no trace of God." To me, this is a beautiful description of non-dual consciousness. Zen master Dogen described it this way: no trace of enlightenment remains, and this no-trace continues on endlessly.

Once, during a ceremony, Zen teacher Mel Weitsman—who, like me, had been instructed by Suzuki Roshi—was asked, "What power will you use to direct others?"

He responded, "When I asked Suzuki Roshi about power, he said 'Don't use it.'"

The questioner pressed on: "Then how will you direct people?"

"You turn me; I'll turn you," Mel said.

The only way to truly walk the spiritual path is together. We can't do it alone. The path isn't fixed; it is winding, frequently doubles back on itself, and often seems to disappear altogether. That's when we rely on others to turn us in the right direction. It takes wakefulness—our own and that of others. Wakefulness is both the medium and the message.

What is the message? You turn me; I'll turn you. This is how we heal ourselves—and our world.

So let's do this together, okay?

Acknowledgments

THANKS TO MY WIFE, LINDA, whom I met at the San Francisco Zen Center fifty-two years ago and who has been the major support person in my life ever since; to my two children, Jed and Erin, and my grandchildren, Ethan and Logan; and to my two dharma teachers, Suzuki Roshi and Katagiri Roshi, who showed me how to unburden myself of the worries and woes that drag so many of us down.

And a special thanks to my editor and friend, Wanda Isle (assisted by Ann Bauleke)—You did it again! Taking a bunch of talks of mine, transcribing them, and artfully molding them to create a meaningful developmental sequence—Wow!

Credits

"Lady Mori's Gifted Touch" by Ikkyu, translated by John Stevens. Used by permission.

"A Man's Root" by Ikkyu, translated by John Stevens. Used by permission.

"A Meal of Fresh Octopus" by Ikkyu, translated by John Stevens. Used by permission.

"No one walks this path . . ." by Basho. Used by permission.

"The old woman was bighearted enough . . ." by Ikkyu, translated by John Stevens. Used by permission.

"Only Breath" by Rumi, from *The Essential Rumi*, translated by Coleman Barks. New York: HarperCollins, 1995. Used by permission.

"Stilted koans . . ." From *Lust for Enlightenment: Buddhism and Sex* by John Stevens. Copyright © 1990 by John Stevens. Reprinted by arrangement with The Permissions Company, Inc., on behalf of Shambhala Publications Inc., Boulder, Colorado, www.shambhala.com.

Excerpt from *Tao Te Ching: The Definitive Edition* by Lao Tzu, translated by Jonathan Star. Translation copyright © 2001 by Jonathan Star. Used by permission of Tarcher, an imprint of Penguin Publishing Group, a division of Penguin Random House LLC. All rights reserved.

"To Lady Mori with Deepest Gratitude and Thanks" by Ikkyu, translated by John Stevens. Used by permission.

"A Woman's Sex" by Ikkyu, translated by John Stevens. Used by permission.

"Year after year" by Basho. Translation copyright © 2011 Jane Hirshfield, from *The Heart of Haiku* (Amazon Single Kindle, 2011); also appears in *Ten Windows: How Great Poems Transform the World* by Jane Hirshfield (Knopf, 2015). Used by permission of Jane Hirshfield. All rights reserved.

Index

"Acornology," 125–26, 128
addictive behaviors
    brain plasticity and, 116–19
    fear-based thinking and, 18
    primary and secondary, 117
    working with, 123, 136
air element, 99, 100
altruism, flow and, 91
American culture
    interdependence and, 54, 55, 129–31
    self-indulgence and, 35–36, 68
    Zen and, 6, 47–48, 54
American Psychological Association, 72
anger
    as trance-inducing veil, 18–19, 22–23
    working with, 23
anxiety
    functions of, 25

    as trance-inducing veil, 19–20, 24–25
    working with, 24
aspiration
    cultivating an abiding, 137
    to realize non-duality, 133
attachment
    ego shell and, 127
    failure without, 65–67
    letting go of, 67
    psychological development and, 127–28
authenticity, humility and, 82–87, 88
avoidance strategies, 19–20
awareness
    flow and, 89, 90, 94
    learning about ourselves and, 141
    mirror neurons and, 122
    nonjudgmental, 25–28, 47
    quarter-second gap and, 135–36

About the Author

 TIM BURKETT began practicing Zen Buddhism in San Francisco in 1964 with the renowned teacher Shunryu Suzuki (author of *Zen Mind Beginner's Mind*). After completing his BA at Stanford University, Tim and his family moved to Minnesota.

Tim's first book, *Nothing Holy About It*, discusses how Zen's core teachings unfold within the ordinary comedies and tragedies of everyday life. In both his books, as in his life, Tim reveals how to live in the world with a deep joy that comes from embracing the work and play of this very moment.

Tim is the former CEO of the largest non-profit in Minnesota for the mentally impaired and chemically dependent. He is a psychologist, a Zen Buddhist priest, and the Guiding Teacher of Minnesota Zen Meditation Center. He and his wife, Linda, have two grown children and two grandchildren.